Profitable
Office
Management
for the
Growing
Business

Profitable Office Management for the Growing Business

Edward N. Rausch

amacom

American Management Associations

10019742

This book is available at a special discount
when ordered in bulk quantities. For information,
contact AMACOM, Special Sales Department,
135 West 50th Street, New York, NY 10020.

Library of Congress Cataloging in Publication Data

Rausch, Edward N.
  Profitable office management for the growing business.

  Includes index.
  1. Office management. I. Title.
HF5547.R282 ~~1983~~ 1984 651.3   83-45210
ISBN 0-8144-5779-7

Printing number
10 9 8 7 6 5 4 3 2 1

To Eloise
for our forty happy years together

Contents

*Profitable
Office
Management
for the
Growing
Business*

INTRODUCTION
The Importance of
Your Office

Because of the complexity of today's expanding business community, there is no such thing as a "typical" growing company office. The scope of activity performed in small to medium-sized offices across the country ranges from thousands of documents, produced by a group of typists who work full time for a month, to the simple "Report of Calls" that a traveling salesman takes fifteen minutes to fill out each evening in his motel room. Either example, plus a myriad of others in between, should be regarded as office work, as long as data are being processed. Thus, office work is being broadly defined: every modern office, large or small, processes data.

To narrow down the subject matter, we might ask "what kind of data?" However, a moment's reflection tells us that countless forms of information are being handled by various offices every day. A more meaningful approach is to ask how the data will be used. In fact, this will be one of the principal themes which this book will address. Relevant questions are: Who will need the data? When and how are the data to be supplied? What are the end purposes of the data? We'll examine all of these questions and develop answers that emphasize *business profitability.*

The major contribution that office work can make toward the profitability of a growing company is not commonly recognized. It is easy to see why and how production work is judged according to its profitability. The same applies to sales activities and the management of business finances. But does the same frame of reference apply to office work? Can clerical output be either profitable or unprofitable? The answer is a resounding "yes." Later, a good many pages will be devoted to discussions of how the data processing performed by your office can be categorized as either profitable or unprofitable.

The other major focus of this book will be the *proper management* of a growing business office. As is the case with many other forms of activity, office management should be regarded as an entity. It can be examined "in isolation." Furthermore, the quality of office management can always be improved. Proficiency in managing a business office of any size can be attained by a person who tries hard enough. All too often, however, office management is inadequate or poorly performed. A principal characteristic of poor office management will always be the failure to make any contribution toward increased business profitability.

Thus, the two primary themes that will be developed in this book are closely related. The profitable use of office data, and the right way to manage your growing office, are simply two separate ways of describing the same thing.

Now, let's turn to an examination of some things that office work *is not*. A few general misconceptions need to be cleared up. Office work is not just red tape. It is not a parasitic business operation, feeding on the rest of the organization. Unfortunately, that's the view many people hold about office work. Admittedly, much of this bad reputation might be deserved, because a business office can be a focal point for some of the most extreme forms of inefficiency or bureaucracy. In such a case, the office work doesn't benefit the organization, and management of such work is definitely improper.

When office work is performed for a profitable purpose, the principal beneficiary is likely to be—the boss, the top management. That's as it should be. Office work ought to be designed, above all else, to help the upper management of the company do a better job. Taking this viewpoint clarifies one basic reason why we have business offices: because bosses need them. Your boss, head of a growing business, needs help from your entire office staff. That's because your growing business is probably still not large enough for you to afford full-time employment of specialists in such office disciplines as the computerization of record-keeping, development of future strategies, or plans for the elimination of waste. If your particular company is to improve in various ways *and become more profitable*, then the source of those improvements will have to come—in part, at least—from your office staff.

This book will address a number of concepts and procedures that are aimed at providing better administrative support and greater profitability of operations—in other words, good management of your small but growing business office. To illustrate particular points, the author will offer many practical examples drawn from his private consulting practice. While the specific situations were encountered among fewer than a hundred firms located in a medium-sized Midwestern city, they are equally applicable to growing offices throughout the country. Office work today is generally similar wherever it takes place. In their detailed particulars, of course, certain clerical activities in your organization may differ greatly from those carried out in other companies. This text will deal only with basic, well-accepted office processes that are common to all business concerns and that possess similar characteristics across the board. The first chapter will begin with that complex system of interrelationships known as the "office organization."

1
Organizing Your Office for Efficient Operation

Your office can't contribute to business profitability if it is poorly organized. The organization plan of any office could logically be compared to the skeleton of an animal. Various functions that the office needs to perform must be grouped and "linked" in much the same way that muscles and bones are fastened together and work to make an animal move. The leverage that your office can exert—the strengths or weaknesses of its operation—are considerably influenced by an underlying organization structure, which may be either effective or inadequate.

Too many small, uncomplicated business offices are composed of a group of clerks and typists who are hired "to take care of our paperwork" and who report in a general way to one or more officers of the company. If a certain office employee seems to have too much to do, several of the others help out. If a new task is decided on, it may be given to the person who otherwise has the least work. If someone is either incompetent or has a "difficult personality," some of that person's duties may be parceled out among other employees in order to avoid trouble. Needless to say, this is no way to run either a railroad or an office. The approach described becomes distinctly detrimental if the business begins to grow and to require more clerical output. It is hoped that your office doesn't fit this description.

Office Organizational Principles

There is nothing so practical as a good organization; few things are so troublesome as an inadequate one. Fortunately, it's never too late to restructure an office of any size in accordance with generally accepted organizational rules that apply to all aspects of business. This is particularly true with respect to a growing office such as yours, which probably is characterized by the addition of more functions, more problems, and more people from time to time.

Think of it this way. Your expanding clerical staff is an integral part of the company. The internal working relationships must be given some consideration and analysis, if the office's overall organization is to make an appropriate contribution to profitability. So this examination of your office organization will begin with a review of a few well-accepted rules. To accomplish the most, the manager of any group should:

- Determine the objectives for that group
- Establish functions, as needed to reach those objectives
- Obtain sufficient personnel to accomplish such functions
- Assign responsibilities to the staff, consistent with the designated functions

Let's consider what it would mean for your office to follow the above four rules. How should you apply them? Well, for a start, has top management established objectives for the business as a whole? There's more involved here than a meeting at the end of the year, where the big boss delivers a pep talk and says, "We're going to make such-and-such amount of money next year." Instead, the entire management group should be thinking in terms of an array of practical long-range goals pointing toward business growth or the expansion of the company's capital. These goals, in turn, must be related to current business income and to the ongoing use of whatever money, property, or equipment the company has been able to accumulate up to now. In other words, the *long-range goals* for the business should involve a spectrum of *short-term (yearly) objectives* set for various parts of the business. For example, there ought to be a yearly sales objective, as well as a set of operating targets related to the company's output, control of costs, number of employees, and so on. Included in this group of targets should be a few office objectives.

Office Objectives

Don't despair if top management hasn't spelled out the office objectives very clearly. Such objectives are seldom specified fully. It's enough if top management tells you how much money you can spend and the scope of other company activities you'll have to support. Even that much information isn't always forthcoming, especially when a company is young and growing rapidly. If the company, as a whole, has rather vague long- and short-term goals, you can still improve office efficiency by developing your own objectives. *Don't* expect to cover every activity of the office, but *do* set some specific performance targets for your major functions, particularly those which are increasing in importance. Any activity which you feel to be especially weak or lacking in orientation should also receive the "target" treatment. (Improving collection of customer accounts and managing inventory more efficiently are the favorites among so many organizations that they could almost be compared with apple pie and motherhood.)

The bulk of office work should be grouped under such "blanket" goals as *hold salary costs constant* or *hold to 5 percent growth in cost of supplies* or *reduce processing time for customer orders*. The principal point to keep in mind is that each and every office objective must be *measurable*. In other words, at the end of the year you should be able to determine (as the result of estimates or record-keeping) how close the office came to attaining every goal.

Fortunately, you can set realistic objectives for a wide range of administrative activities. For example, an ambitious manager of the author's acquaintance recently decided to improve the performance and development of every worker in her office. After considerable study, she set numeric goals that the output of each worker had to reach. As a part of this project, standards had to be established for a whole host of office tasks. Typing keystrokes, the number of cards processed by a bookkeeping machine, the addressing of plate impressions—all these things and many more were standardized. This example illustrates how far a comprehensive or "blanket" objective (in this case, improvement of workers' performance) can penetrate into various office activities. So it is highly worthwhile to do a thorough job of defining an array of short-range targets.

Office Functions

The next step in the organizing process is to identify all of the office functions that will be affected by the objectives that you've set (or that have been sent down to you by top management.) A skeptic could consider all of this a superfluous process. Your office is already "in being." The workers have tasks assigned to them. Why go to the trouble of grouping these tasks into so-called functions? There are a number of benefits from doing so. When you give a name to a complete office function—say, "collection of customer accounts"—this provides (1) sharper definition of the various office jobs, and (2) clearly established "boundaries" for each. The utility of these benefits will become more significant to you later in the chapter, when we discuss departmentalization through grouping of related functions.

If you've never gone through the exercise of ferreting out all of the functions now taking place in your office, you may be in for a shock. Typically, an office manager is unaware of a good many jobs that are being performed in his or her growing office. Some of these may even be obsolete—having come to life from a directive issued when the office was smaller. But you'll never know about those things unless you take the trouble to "inventory" all the functions of your office. So this points to another possible benefit of well-defined office functions—the elimination of unnecessary work.

For each short-term objective, you need to *decide what must be done* and then find out *who is doing it*. Here again, you may uncover more "pay dirt." Occasionally it is discovered that someone is assigned to perform only part of a function, so that another employee must finish it. Or two people may be duplicating each other's work. Or perhaps successive functional steps are being done at some physical distance from each other. And so on and so on.

The Office Organization Plan

The reason why such undesirable and inefficient activities begin to develop in a growing office can be traced to one very common fault—the lack of a *formal organization plan*. Let's examine two reasons why your office should have a preconsidered plan:

1. To show the relationship of the various clerical functions being carried out
2. To illustrate the comparative status or importance of those functions, as well as the "rank" of each person who is responsible for seeing that a given function is performed

Suppose, for example, that a certain business office performs fifteen different functions, which serve the entire company. These are:

1. Message center (telephone switchboard and distribution of mail)
2. Maintenance of personnel records
3. Typing pool

4. Payroll and tax record-keeping
5. Inventory record-keeping
6. Customer accounts record-keeping
7. Payment for goods and services purchased
8. Custodian of cash
9. Acceptance of customer orders
10. Issuance of bills and statements
11. Maintenance of sales representatives' commission records
12. Preparation of production orders
13. Photocopy center
14. Messenger service
15. Receptionist

Note that in the above list, the functions and responsibilities of some management members, such as the accountant and the purchasing agent, have been omitted. However, these individuals occasionally require clerical assistance from the office, so we'll add one more function.

16. Administrative support

In reading down the list of functions (which purposely have been somewhat scrambled), an "outsider"—someone not directly connected with the office—wouldn't know which are most important or which are interrelated. Furthermore, there are logically several ways that some office functions could be grouped, depending on the nature of the business, its size, and what kinds of goods or services are being dispensed. However, if you take the time to chart a formal plan (see Figure 1 for an example), a number of these uncertainties are easily resolved.

From Figure 1 we know, for example, that the assistant to the president is responsible for managing all office activities at the Acme Products Company, and that he has three key subordinate supervisors whose areas of authority are roughly equal.

Figure 1. Acme Products—office organization plan.

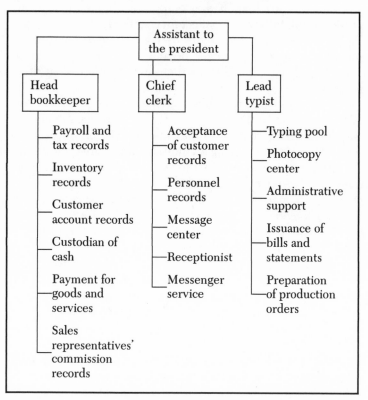

We can understand why the functions are subdivided in the manner indicated, although it would certainly be possible to set up some different arrangement. (Departmentalization will be discussed more fully later in the chapter.) Finally, we know that if there is a disagreement between, for example, the person who is custodian of cash and the payroll clerk, this disagreement should be settled by the head bookkeeper. In a different situation, if the typist who issues bills and statements has a conflict with the person who maintains customer account records, the head bookkeeper and the lead typist would try to arbitrate the problem. If they could not, the assistant to the president might have to make a final settlement.

To conclude this discussion, here are some common-sense rules for setting up an office organization plan. These principles have been applied many times in the author's consulting practice:

1. *Closely related functions should be linked whenever possible.* For instance, Figure 1 shows a variety of document origination functions that are under the supervision of the head typist. Functions involving accounting entries are grouped under the head bookkeeper. Other miscellaneous clerical functions are supervised by the chief clerk. The first two aspects of this particular plan (responsibilities of the head typist and head bookkeeper) are especially significant because of future changes that might be made. The origination of specific records might be shifted from one function to another if new conditions arise outside the office. The almost inevitable introduction of an electronic computer into the office (with its capacity of performing different kinds of data processing) would give the head bookkeeper an opportunity gradually to combine most of his or her accounting functions into one centralized activity.

2. *Ease of administrative supervision should be facilitated.* Not only should administrators have comprehensive knowledge of the work performed in different functional areas, but they can benefit from the enhanced visual control provided by a "line of sight" arrangement. For example, if the physical facilities of the office permit it, the lead typist should ensure that all document-preparation functions are located close together in one area. This arrangement would enable him or her to scan all activities visually. Another approach to improving administrative control might be to have the head bookkeeper use an accounting "entry trail" (such as all payroll or accounts receivable processing) to establish proper grouping of functions.

3. *Simplicity should be much preferred to complexity.* For example, the organization plan shown in Figure 1 could have

been established with additional key subordinates reporting to the assistant to the president. Presently, each of the three subordinate supervisors has been charged with a mixed bag of functions. However, even in an office that is growing rapidly, there is no excuse for a complicated plan with an overabundance of bosses. It's better to assign each supervisor some functions that are only marginally related to his or her principal duties. Remember that *organization plans are not necessarily permanent*. They should be reviewed from time to time and changed whenever the size of the office has increased significantly or the mix of functions performed in the office has been modified substantially.

Assigned Accountability for Office Functions

In the two chapters that follow this one, we'll devote a good deal of attention to the question of how personnel in the office should be administered and controlled. Yet the basic point can be expressed in a single sentence: *some key supervisor should be made accountable for each office function and should see to it that the work is properly performed*. You know that; unless you're just starting as an office manager, you've probably given such assignments to your supervisors many times. But have you ever considered the question: Can every person effectively supervise the same amount of office activity (that is, have the same span of control)? Unfortunately, the answer is no. What's more, there's no simple rule to help you decide how many supervisory functions should be included under any person's span of control. In fact, your final decision should be conditioned by many factors. Some considerations are:

- A few supervisors might have greater administrative ability, sensitivity, and stability than their peers.
- Most supervisors improve with experience and respond well if you "stretch" them with increasingly difficult assignments.
- Some office work is more important or more complex, thereby justifying more supervisory attention.

- Talented workers need much less supervision than workers with mediocre ability.
- The physical arrangement of the office can be a factor. For instance, if office work is performed on several different floors of a building (or simply in several rooms), a more stringent degree of supervision may be warranted.

For all of the above reasons, it's impossible to set fixed limits for the span of supervisory control in your office. The most that can be said is that this span ought to be proportionate to (1) the nature of the work being performed, (2) the abilities of your supervisors, and (3) the size and layout of the office. Depending on the number of available capable people and the nature of your office, the most effective hierarchy of supervision can be described either as "tall" or "flat" or as somewhere in between. The two extremes are illustrated in Figure 2.

As noted earlier, every office function must be made the prime concern of some supervisor. Certainly no function should be split between supervisors. Instead, the trick is to *group related functions* that a growing office must perform, and also to decide what boundaries should be set for each supervisor. Once these decisions are made, your only remaining concern is to be sure that the proper people have been designated as supervisors, and that they use appropriate techniques. This matter will be discussed at greater length in Chapter 3.

However, determining what each supervisor should be held accountable for is just half the battle. You also must be concerned with the tasks that the workers themselves are supposed to perform. Only by deciding what both parties will do can you ensure a really effective office operation.

Work Subdivision Related to Office Organization

When trying for the best assignment of office labor, it may be helpful for you to think of the work as a matrix of clusters, or "work cells," that are linked together. Each cell is distinct, yet

Figure 2.   Possible configurations of office organization plans.

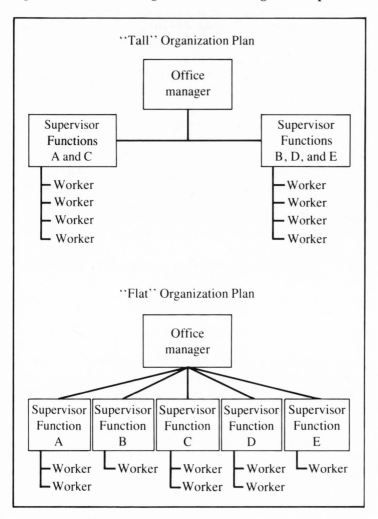

each can be related to one or more other cells. Also, a work cell need not be of any particular size. For instance, if your company processes a considerable number of individual customer orders, then *order acceptance* could be an identifiable work cell. However, if several employees handle each order, a further breakdown into two smaller cells may be appropriate. Let's say that two people open the mail and check the order "specs" against a catalogue; another worker then proceeds to perform the mathematics of price times quantity minus discount plus tax. In such a situation, you have two work cells within the general function of *order acceptance*. This example is typical of dozens of discrete work subdivisions usually found in a small to medium-sized office that is growing.

If you categorize work in this way, then the content of individual jobs can be related to your office organization plan. To determine how this can best be accomplished, it is helpful first to get down to basics. For example, effective organizing of any office requires that every employee have a *definite set of assigned tasks*—work that is he finds recognizable and understandable, and can carry out on his own without direction. That's a basic fact of office life. But should all of the important work in your office be divided up at the individual worker level? Or should some kinds of work be assigned to groups rather than individuals? Furthermore, what kinds of work should be allocated to particular individuals? The basic answer to all of these questions is: it depends on the nature of the work. For greatest profitability of operations, the potential of either job specialization, job enrichment, or job centralization deserves to be investigated.

Job Specialization

Past experience has shown that some types of office work must be specialized for the sake of efficiency. Complex office tasks need to be broken down into relatively simple "cells" that workers can easily learn how to do. In this way, the cost of training employees can be reduced. Each worker more quickly becomes expert in his or her limited area of operation.

Also, if your office is mechanized or if you foresee enough growth to justify mechanization, then specialization becomes a "must" with respect to the operators of the office machines. When you have a skilled machine operator on the payroll, you don't want such a person to be licking stamps or stuffing envelopes. Furthermore, *no person can do everything equally well*. Why not capitalize on an employee's manual dexterity, analytical ability, capacity for detecting typographical errors, or other special skill? In short, in a growing office, many types of clerical work can be more efficiently accomplished when the jobs are specialized.

Unfortunately, there is a direct relationship between the growth of work specialization and a proliferation of those numerous boring routines that many employees find distasteful. Sometimes remedies such as "background music," scheduled rest periods, and job rotation can help to offset the monotony of the work. These measures may be especially appropriate if a good many of the jobs in your office are becoming highly specialized.

Job Enrichment

In your particular case, there might be only a marginal degree of profitability to be derived from specializing most of the office jobs. (This is most likely if the office is still relatively small.) Further, some members of your present clerical staff may become potential candidates for advancement as the office continues to grow. If that reason figures in your thinking, or if you simply wish to enhance office work satisfaction, then you should look at some alternatives to job specialization. The many possibilities that are generally described by the term "job enrichment" deserve to be investigated.

Job enrichment involves expansion of office jobs in a variety of ways to make them more challenging and therefore less distasteful. Job enrichment can be described in terms of the "work cell" concept explained earlier. The assignment of more than one cell to the same person (or a group of cells to a team of workers) increases the variety of an office worker's duties, and cuts down on the monotony. Even if the tasks are relatively simple and are closely related, employees will tend to appreciate such special consideration. *This is particularly true if the job changes are accompanied by a convincing presentation from management*, explaining the reason for the job-enrichment program. In several cases among the author's consulting clientele, such an explanation was originally omitted, with unfavorable consequences. The workers perceived the management as simply trying to get more work from a staff of the same size, and the whole plan backfired. In each of these situations, it took a concentrated program of meetings and written communications to overcome the suspicions created by management's well-intended but initially misguided efforts.

Job enrichment, when properly instituted, enhances the attractiveness of office work. The usual result is an increase in output, reduced wastage of material, and decreased absenteeism—benefits that obviously increase the profitability of operations. Clearly, job enrichment is an important possibility for you to consider. However, an ill-conceived or poorly developed enrichment program can create more problems than benefits. You need to weigh the alternatives very carefully.

Job Centralization

Another facet of work subdivision has to do with the centralization versus decentralization of certain work in your office. Should all kinds of typing, for instance, be processed by a pool of typists? Should a variety of record-keeping functions be channeled through an electronic computer? Or should every kind of work be processed in a different way, in various parts of the office, as the need arises? Here are some pros and cons for you to consider:

Advantages of office work centralization

- Through centralizing, it becomes possible to minimize peaks and valleys in the flow of office work.
- Centralization is compatible with work standardization.

- Work output can be measured more easily if it is all performed in one place.
- Duplication of effort and/or equipment can be eliminated (or at the very least reduced) when the work is centralized.

Advantages of office work decentralization

- It is easier to prioritize work if various work elements are not merged.
- Better accountability will result when special work is separately carried out.
- Decentralization encourages a feeling of worker responsibility.
- Control over "confidential" work is greatly improved, since it can be segregated more easily.

Where work centralization exists, there should be a written set of rules or procedures to be followed. These free the department supervisor from the need to direct and redirect work routines constantly. Also, the rules or procedures create greater predictability or consistency; in short, work efficiency will usually increase. However, despite these potential benefits, growing offices are generally *not* centralized. There should be a reason why so few office managers have chosen the centralization option—and, apparently, there is. Many managers seem to feel that decentralization makes for greater ease of operation. If all work has to be done "by the book"—that is, always carried out according to a prescribed procedure—the prevailing opinion is that a given set of activities will take longer to get done. This attitude may be a holdover from the days when offices were smaller and life was simpler. Is it an attitude that you share?

Without question, decentralized operations allow workers to find shortcuts and possibly to increase their output. Many employees prefer this because they develop a greater degree of interest and sense of participation in the course of performing their work. As a result, decentralized workers can become more motivated and more satisfied with their jobs. However, take note that an incompetent worker can get by more easily (for a time) with errors or lack of production in a decentralized office.

As with many aspects of office organization, there is no ideal type of work subdivision. The method (or methods) selected for your growing office should be conditioned by (1) the diversity of your operations, and (2) the stability of your activity. If the office is quite diverse—that is, if *many different functions* must be performed—decentralization and job enrichment could be your best choices. On the other hand, if *relatively few functions* are performed in your office, job specialization and centralization of work might be better, at least for your major activities. Work in a *constantly changing* office probably should be subdivided following the same guidelines as for a highly diverse office. By way of contrast, if the office activities are *fairly stable*, consider job specialization and centralization.

Popular Approaches to Office Departmentalization

Any organization (including your growing office) that is composed of a number of people will spontaneously develop both an informal hierarchy and a "structure" in which every person finds a place. This development is a natural result of the interplay among various personalities within the office, as well as their activities and conflicts. Whether or not you personally have been aware of it, this has already happened in your office and is generally recognized by all except the newest of the employees. But an important question remains: Will this so-called informal hierarchy and structure be compatible with the overall purpose of your office, or could these developments work against accomplishment of your objectives? If such a question seems either theoretical or silly to you, stop and think for a minute. Do you really know how the people in your office interrelate as they work together? Do you know the identity of the one or more informal leaders among the staff, whose influence appears to be considerable, whose opinion seems to count in most cases, and whose approval is frequently sought? There will certainly be several employees like that in your office. What's more, these people may not always agree with your decisions; they may, in fact, sometimes work at cross purposes to you.

The best remedy for a growing office with such a control problem is to set up a well-thought-out and properly designed *formal hierarchy and structure*. If this is done, you will have a solid line of defense against either reluctant compliance or downright defiance on the part of some employees.

Hierarchical Concepts

Every office has certain clerical functions to perform, and someone must be directed to see that each function is carried out. Such a person, then, is considered to be in charge of particular work, and certain terms have been developed to describe what he or she does. In the subsequent discussion we will be using the following terms, with their meanings to be understood as follows:

1. *Authority* is the right of a person to act or to make a decision.
2. This authority is *delegated* (passed down) from the head of the organization to his or her subordinates. (In an office, the "office manager" is commonly the title of the organization head, and "department supervisor" or "section head" is a title frequently given to the immediate subordinates of the office manager.)
3. There are two universal types of authority—*line* and *staff*.
4. Authority is not the same as *responsibility*; the meaning of latter is synonymous with "accountability."

A few more words of explanation about authority and responsibility are in order. The responsibilities of an office department supervisor are all of the things he or she is obligated to take care of—things like quantity of output or level of expenses, or perhaps proper conduct of the workers. The authority of that department supervisor is the power or the right to see that those responsibilities are fulfilled.

No matter how much or how little authority has been assigned, a department supervisor's authority is always augmented (or decreased) by behavior and appearance on the job. Naturally, what a person knows about the work helps to enhance his or her authority. So does his or her manner of dress. The ability to be persuasive and the nature of the supervisor's work habits are also quite influential. All of these supplemental qualities possessed by the department supervisor become apparent to subordinates as they go about their everyday duties. In terms of gaining cooperation from employees, looking and acting like a boss is often just as important as the actual scope of a position. In other words, your formal delegation of responsibility and authority is not sufficient; you should require in addition that your key subordinates learn how to "play the part."

While both authority and responsibility must be delegated (they flow down from your office, as previously stated), they should always be delegated *in parallel*. Otherwise, one of your department supervisors could be made responsible for some aspect of the work but might have no control (authority) over it. Conversely, if you assign a department supervisor some area of authority (power) but no specific kinds of responsibility, you may find that you have a monster on your hands. The one basic fact behind this delegation puzzle is that a delegated responsibility never really leaves the domain of the delegator. For this reason, many bosses are reluctant to delegate any important responsibility to a subordinate. The responsibility that is passed down can quickly come back to haunt the delegator if the person who receives that responsibility doesn't use it properly. In other words, responsibility that has been passed down can also flow in the opposite direction, *up the chain of command*, when something goes wrong. However, this is no reason to steer away from delegating altogether.

Finally, the distinction between line and staff authority needs to be specified:

- *Line authority.* A department supervisor with this type of authority generally is directly in control of some office function. Such a supervisor is thought of as a "boss." He or she normally has subordinates and sees that office output is generated.
- *Staff authority.* Persons with this type of authority may not supervise anyone, and may have special titles that describe their unique skills. They usually provide some kind of professional advice or expertise. Their duty is to assist people who have line authority in a variety of ways.

In a small but growing office, line and staff authority may very well reside in the same person. Frequently, one department head "wears two hats," with titles such as supervisor of duplicating (line) and office supply buyer (staff). There are, of course, a thousand and one ways to create an office organization plan. Thus, there are also a thousand and one possible combinations of supervisory authority.

Some readers may wonder what all this hierarchical theory is leading up to—how it can be used to get more work done. The answer is that hierarchical concepts help in *dividing work into easily supervised units.* By doing a good job of delegating office work, and the necessary responsibility and authority over such work, you can improve efficiency and reduce costs. An effective office department generally has a well-thought-out formal hierarchy and structure.

Office Departmentalization Possibilities

Earlier in this chapter, when office functions were under consideration, we touched upon *linking of such functions* into an actual office department. In fact, that approach is one of the three most frequently used to increase profitability. The three possibilities are as follows:

Departmentalizing by function or activity
Departmentalizing by type of output or service
Departmentalizing by geographic location

Obviously, the choice must be left to you. You know your own organization best. You know what demands must be met, and what constraints will be imposed. You may also be inclined to experiment with changes in organization from time to time, in an effort to improve efficiency.

With regard to departmentalization, two points are especially applicable to growing offices. First of all, because growth will bring about frequent changes in functional scope or office size, *the current mode of office departmentalization should be reviewed every year.* Usually, some realignment will seem desirable. Second, *the ways in which functional responsibility and authority are assigned are a reflection of the supervisor in charge.* What's more, people change in accordance with their experience and the pressure exerted on them. The structure of a department and the way it operates can vary over time in accordance with the growth or stagnation of the supervisor who heads it up. Since change is inevitable, nothing is sacred when it comes to the boundaries of departments included in an office organization plan.

To test the viability of current departmentalization within your growing office, consider these three points:

• When the functional approach has been followed, office work requiring *similar* equipment, knowledge, or skills is frequently merged into a single department. This is consistent with work centralization, and provides the previously described advantages and drawbacks. Check to make sure that the advantages dominate.

• By deciding to departmentalize according to geographic location or according to type of output or service, you may create *duplication* of functions, equipment, or experience among different departments. This can result in an increase in costs. You should make sure that the benefits derived from selecting either of these two approaches to departmentalization offset the additional costs.

• Most growing offices should contain departments that have been formed in two or even all three of the ways described above. It would be a mistake to insist that every department in the same office follow only one plan.

The Significance of People in Office Organizations

So far, this chapter has focused on abstract principles of office organization. While formal organization is important, in the real world, individual personnel also make a great contribution to the progress of the office. People—not procedures or policies or equipment—are always the principal ingredients of offices. They constitute the "glue" that holds everything together and makes it operate. People have needs, experiences, and conflicts. They react to office work in keeping with their inclinations and ambitions.

The combined impact of all the people in an office will have a substantial influence on what organizational design should be chosen. It is fitting to acknowledge this significance and to "build a bridge" between this chapter and the two that follow. It goes without saying that every organization must set limits and requirements for its working staff. Otherwise, the organization will fail. (Imagine what would happen in your office, for example, if the employees did whatever work they wanted to do and for only the number of hours that pleased them.) Obviously, an organization must demand conformity to rules from its employees. But what about demands *upon the organization, stemming from the working force?* These latter demands are often of equal importance.

There has always been a variety of expectations that an office manager and his organization have had to satisfy in order to attract capable employees and keep them from quitting once they have been hired. Employees want adequate pay, tolerable working conditions, useful work, and so on. For as long as people have been gainfully employed, these characteristics of a work environment have been attractive. Today, however, there are a few new complications.

The so-called work ethic that motivated many office workers of a generation ago—that is, a desire to find intrinsic satisfaction in their work apart from financial compensation—is still important to many people. They expect their jobs to provide a sense of purpose and of self-worth. To the extent that this desire is met, an individual is fulfilled; to the extent that the desire is frustrated, an individual is both disappointed and unproductive. In a profitable office, there must be much concern for the upgrading of worker morale.

It is notable, however, that the work ethic appears to have a somewhat reduced significance. Although people still want to do interesting and challenging work, the idea of "exchange" has become prevalent. "If you do such and such for me, I'll do such and such for you. But I won't put out extra effort unless you pay extra money." As a result, an individual's performance on the job currently is dependent on three prime variables: (1) the extent of his or her ability, (2) good working conditions and intrinsically satisfying work, and (3) whether there appears to be a fair exchange of work and compensation. It is important for every office manager to understand this. In organizing your office, you must give due recognition to the needs and values of the workers. If you neglect these things, your people will neglect you.

Conclusion

Your expanding office, and its organization and structure, represent an important element of the entire company. Other parts of the business are always affected by office operations. So your decisions become very important. How should authority and responsibility be distributed? How should jobs and people be grouped? What functions are needed to meet the office objectives that have been set? Are there enough rewarding types of work to keep the employees happy?

No matter what your growing office is like today, it should be flexible enough to accommodate changes tomorrow. From time to time, you need to review how your office is organized to ensure that it really is operating efficiently and profitably. Assistance in making such a determination is the kind of help that this book is designed to provide.

2
Handling Administration of Your Office Personnel

The people who work in your office can be considered in two entirely different ways:

- As elements in the assemblage of productive assets, which have been acquired to turn out the work of the office
- As sensitive and unique individuals who have talents, aspirations, feelings, faults, and all of the other human "cargo" that each of us carries throughout our working careers

This chapter will deal only with the first consideration; the next chapter will explore the second.

Converting Office Objectives into Estimated Personnel Needs

In the preceding chapter, the "translation" of objectives into office functions was discussed. In a similar manner, it is possible to proceed from a statement of office goals to reach a ballpark conclusion regarding the personnel required to attain those goals. Figure 3 briefly indicates the various steps that are involved. The diagrammed approach suggests that there is a *direct relationship* between what you expect the office to accomplish, and the kinds and numbers of people needed if all those goals are to be reached. Obviously, this plan for staffing is an ideal rather than exact method. When you consider the implementation of the plan, several deficiencies quickly come to mind:

Figure 3. Office personnel administrative plan.

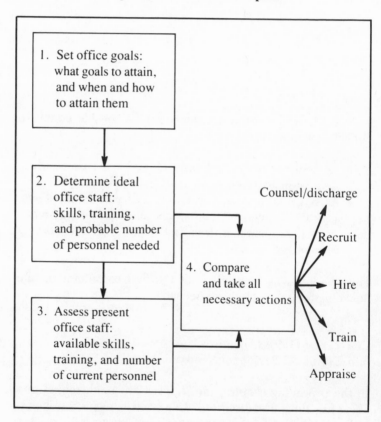

- It is very difficult to "quantify" office objectives accurately, in order to achieve a realistic estimate of personnel needs.
- Office objectives frequently change. Thus, selecting the most desirable office staff is like hitting the bull's-eye of a moving target, insofar as numbers of people and types of ability are concerned.
- The characteristics and talents of present employees cannot always be readily inventoried.
- The opinions of any personnel "appraiser" who would determine the adequacy of the present staff would be subjective and thus susceptible to influence by personal biases.

Despite the above objections, one prime advantage of developing an estimated office personnel staffing plan stands out: *such a plan can be very cost-effective.* The remainder of this chapter will be devoted to a discussion of how such a plan can be set up and administered. Even if only partially successful, the effort can have a substantial payoff in profitability for your office. Here's how to begin:

1. *Analyze the office work.* You or someone reporting to you know exactly what the primary functions are in your office. That is, you do if you've followed the recommendations given in Chapter 1. Ask yourself: How much work must be generated by each function in order to achieve the office objectives?

2. *Attempt to break the necessary work down into total "work hours."* This can best be done by making a careful estimate of *time required for a unit of output for each major function.* In each department, get help from a senior office worker or department supervisor, if at all possible. Be sure to make the estimate in terms of *work hours.* Note: Where an office job is mechanized, this estimate is fairly easy to obtain. It is simply the average machine output, converted into units per hour. But don't forget to allow for set-up time and possible machine repairs. (In the section on formal work scheduling in Chapter 4, you'll find another approach to obtaining estimates of work hours for large-volume jobs.)

3. *Total the number of work hours per function and divide by the number of hours in a standard workweek.* This calculation produces the number of employees needed per office function.

4. *Add to this total the following two "fudge factors"*: (a) the number of all "indirect" workers needed to perform such functions as receptionist, messenger, telephone answering, mail distribution, office housekeeping, and any other activities that are not directly productive but are necessary to keep the office in operation; (b) an extra allowance to accommodate absences, tardiness, holidays, and vacations. This allowance is fairly easy to determine. You simply calculate how many work hours you lose for each function in a typical month, as a result of all of the above unproductive time off, and convert these "lost" hours into number of employees.

5. Since you already know the primary functions performed in the office, *you simply total the estimated worker requirements per function*, and you have the optimum number of office employees needed.

An example of these basic calculations is shown in the box opposite.

Although the steps are quite straightforward, a few things should be pointed out. First of all, as indicated in these examples, your totals per function will often indicate a fraction of a worker. Usually, you won't be able to hire such a part-person. Also, there will surely be some minor functions that you haven't allowed for in making the estimates that have just been explained. Both of these situations would indicate that a few extra people ought to be added to the staff. However, don't overlook the possibility of cross-trained workers who can be switched readily between functions. This should be possible for a number of the less demanding office activities.

Try to be as realistic as possible in establishing your optimum office force. It's a mistake to be either overstaffed or understaffed by more than one or two people. Then, the next step is to compare what you feel is reasonable with the present group of employees. If you've been a good manager (and also a bit lucky), there will be a close resemblance between the

---

Sample Calculations of Estimated Personnel Requirements

Primary function: Hand-post data on file cards
Time per unit: 1.2 minutes
Number of units per 40-hour week: 2,250 max.; 2,000 min.
Total time required: 1,875 minutes max.;
                            1,667 minutes min.
                                 or
                            31.25 hours max.;
                            27.78 hours min.
Number of
  employees needed: $31.25 \div 40$ = no more than .78
                          $27.78 \div 40$ = no fewer than .69

Primary function: keypunch cards
Time per unit: .225 minutes
Number of units per 40-hour week: 800 max.; 650 min.
Total time required: 3,556 minutes max.;
                            2,889 minutes min.;
                                 or
                            59.27 hours max.;
                            48.15 hours min.
Number of
  employees needed: $59.27 \div 40$ = no more than 1.48
                          $48.15 \div 40$ = no fewer than 1.2

---

number of employees you have estimated are needed and the number of employees now on the payroll. If the disparity is great, however, a variety of personnel administration activities are called for. These will be discussed during the remainder of this chapter. You might want to refer again to Figure 3, to refresh your memory as to the various steps recommended, as well as their sequence. One more suggestion: Try to plan personnel needs as far into the future as possible. It's expensive to constantly juggle the size of the staff by hiring and then laying off, or vice versa, unless there is a long-term trend pointing in one direction or the other.

Now let's turn our attention to the various remedial measures that you can take to "balance" the present work force against the number calculated to be needed to achieve desired objectives.

Counseling the Problem Employee

It might seem logical to recommend that any employee be terminated as soon as he begins to be more of a problem than he is worth. However, this approach is not appropriate until several important corrective activities have been completed. There are some good reasons for taking these remedial steps:

- We are discussing people here, not machines. Therefore, there are humanitarian reasons for going slow when a firing is being considered.
- Also, the employee in question presumably had some value to the office at one time (i.e., before he fell into the problem category). Thus, it might be possible to "salvage" that person and to reclaim any residual value that he still possesses.
- If many unfair terminations take place, the other employees' regard for management and the company's standing in the community will both lose some luster.

On the other hand, your office is no better than the total contribution which every person who works there is capable of. Any unsatisfactory personnel will diminish the organization; it's up to you (or someone delegated by you) to try to avoid this by taking some positive measures. The measures fall under the general category of employee coaching and counseling.

Identifying a Problem Employee

Make no mistake, office workers know who the problem employees are. To try to work with one is to find out very quickly. But very often, *the boss doesn't know*. There are several reasons for this:

- Generally, in every office an unwritten but well-understood "code of silence" is observed by practically all nonmanagement personnel. Succinctly, this code can be expressed as follows: "Don't rat on me when I make a mistake or goof off, and I won't rat on you for the same." Although this attitude virtually amounts to a conspiracy among the working staff, very little can be done about it. The management must find other ways to identify problem employees.
- Poor supervisory controls will permit unsatisfactory performance on the part of workers to go undetected for a long time. This will be discussed in the chapter that follows.
- Lack of work-output information (generally the non-availability of historical records) will make it difficult or impossible to separate good from bad workers. This matter will be considered at some length in Chapter 4, "Controlling the Output of Your Office."

But for the present, let's say that in some fashion you've determined just who the problem employees are. That's fine and it's an essential first step, but now something must be done with this information, and some member of management must be the person to do it.

Counseling Procedures

Nobody enjoys a counseling session—not the counselee (the one being counseled) and certainly not the counselor (the one who has to do the dirty work). However, a rule of thumb that applies here is: the more *ineffective* the counseling session becomes, the more *unenjoyable* it is. In other words, the least objectionable sessions are those which are done properly. And the worst thing you can do is to give the impression that the whole effort is a bad joke, intended merely to find a reason to fire the person. No, a counseling session should be what the name implies—a genuine effort to try to find out what is wrong and to do something about the difficulty. Here are some simple rules to follow:

1. A counseling session is not the time to debate whether the employee's past actions were "right" or "wrong." Don't get trapped into arguing with the employee.
2. Frequently, a problem employee can't—or won't—say what the real reason is for his or her unsatisfactory performance. The counselor must probe from various angles and look for hidden meanings.
3. Listening on the part of the counselor is as important as (and often more important than) talking. Also, concentration is imperative. That means no phone calls, no other visitors, no signing of letters or rearranging of papers on the desk, and so on.
4. One of the worst ways to proceed with counseling is to start by saying, "Now when I have a problem like yours, what I do is. . . ." In other words, don't take a superior attitude. Just be glad you're not on the other side of the desk.
5. Above all, don't offer to solve a particular problem for the person who has it. He got into the mess; he must get himself out of it. The most you can do is try to help.

Probable Counseling Results

One thing that probably *won't* happen is a dramatic turn-around on the part of the employee being counseled. Very often, unsatisfactory performance or behavior has become habitual. Thus, it will be hard for the employee to change overnight. Also, that employee isn't likely to be helped by the counseling session unless he can get some things out in the open—can unburden himself, so to speak. If he finally begins to trust you enough to talk about his frustrations, then slowly, very slowly, his attitude may change and the problem should begin to diminish.

The Belief that Counseling Helps

Because of the unpleasant nature of this duty, it is always a good idea to try to adopt a positive mental attitude. For example, if you're going to do the counseling, here are some things you can say to yourself:

1. Remember you're not prying out some dark secret. All you want are the facts of the matter from the person involved.
2. This is your job. Duties like this go along with some of the privileges you enjoy. So grin and bear it.
3. More than anything else, try to avoid losing your temper or becoming emotionally upset. You can expect that the employee being counseled will react emotionally—they almost always do—and very little can be accomplished if both parties go out of control.
4. Finally, don't think of yourself as a miracle worker. Quite often the problem won't be capable of being solved, and termination may be the only answer.

Recruiting Office Employees

Do you have any idea what it costs to put an employee on your office payroll? Although such a cost obviously varies with circumstances, the total expense for a new hire will probably exceed $4,000—$5,000 by the time the individual's salary during the probation period, plus selection and training costs, are reckoned with. Furthermore, for a growing company, the recruits who are selected this year could be a vital part of the larger organization in three or four years. So, you can readily see that the employment recruiting process is a highly important activity in order for an office to be both effective and profitable.

Attracting Potential Employees

The question of how to attract good candidates for job openings is the first of many problems to be solved. Realistically, every potential employee should be given an accurate picture of the position to be filled, and the nature of the company. A disenchanted "new hiree" is likely to leave at the first opportunity, and often this occurs after considerable training cost has been incurred. Thus, there is an imperative need for candor about future career possibilities and realism regarding working conditions. Also, don't bank too heavily on some *future* training possibility when selecting a candidate. You can't always tell whether an untrained person "could easily learn this job after a few months with the company." It's better to pick a recruit who could learn to perform *right now*.

Legal Complications

Depending on the laws of your state, and especially if your company is engaged in interstate commerce, you might feel completely overwhelmed by some of the legal requirements surrounding personnel hiring. These are primarily the result of legislation designed to protect minority groups and women. You should investigate the specific laws applicable to your company and then consider the following:

1. It is often advisable to advertise job openings in some newspaper or other publication that is read chiefly by minorities. Of course that would be *in addition* to the ad you place in a newspaper that has broader circulation.
2. Take care to avoid designing jobs in your office in such a way that they are most likely to appeal primarily either to minorities or to white males. The job should be as "neutral" as possible—that is, capable of being filled by anyone.
3. It's illegal for you to refuse to hire anyone because of their race, religion, sex, national origin, or age. (It's also illegal to fire anyone for any of the above reasons or to discriminate against any member of a minority group insofar as pay or promotion is concerned.)
4. You *can* use employment tests in selecting employees that might exclude either minorities or women, but you must be able to prove that these tests relate to a specific job under consideration rather than to a group of jobs.

5. Finally, it's illegal to advertise for job openings or to include questions on your employment application form in which language is used that is discriminatory in any way. The same applies to interviewing.

Following are some guidelines for "equal employment" interviewing. Questions that probe any of the following areas can be interpreted as infringing on a person's equal right to employment:

Religion
Race
National origin
Sex
Age
Marital status

Questions covering the following should stay within indicated limits, to avoid possible infringement:

- Citizenship. You may ask whether the person is an American citizen or has legal permanent residence, but nothing beyond that.
- Disability. You may discuss any current disability that would interfere with the work. You may not ask about prior disabilities.
- Criminal record. An arrest is not cause for denying employment unless the business would be affected. A conviction is sufficient cause, and you may ask about it.
- Physical strength. You may ask about this only if the job entails heaving, lifting, pushing, or pulling.

The Selection Process

You will be looking for an applicant to fill a specific job, and will want to choose the candidate who will probably be best suited to the kind of work in question. Depending on how selective you want to be, the following steps are suggested:

1. Use a formal application form, and screen all of the completed forms before you interview the applicants.
2. A personal interview by the department supervisor is a must. Sometimes, interviews by several other office administrators are a good idea.
3. Have someone *personally* check all references. Most letters of recommendation are so general that they don't apply to specific jobs under consideration.
4. In many jobs, a physical examination is very important. The same may apply to some type of psychological testing. These things cost money, but bear in mind what it would cost to hire, train, and then later discharge an unsuitable employee.

Hiring Office Employees

The actual hiring process requires very little comment in comparison to training (which will be discussed next). However, there are common deficiencies that the author frequently finds in offices which are part of growing companies. These deficiencies are:

1. Very often, new employees don't know the office rules or the fringe benefits of employment. A simple booklet (or a few typed pages) would be sufficient to correct this condition. It is always worth the time and effort to compile this type of handout, because a new employee can be negatively influenced by the lack of such information. Studies show that most new employees have lower morale during the first month on the job than at any other time in their tenure.

2. New employees should always go through a probationary period. You can never be 100 percent sure that a proper selection has been made. There are invariably some unexpected aspects associated with bringing a new person into the office. The best way to avoid trouble, when an employee is being considered for termination within a month or two after being hired, is to have preestablished a ninety-day probation period that everyone goes through. During that time, it should be possible to fire the person without any first or second warn-

ing and without the person having the right to any legal recourse against the office.

Training Office Employees

Probably the most important single influence that your office could exert on any employee is his or her initial training. If training is poor, the employee may either quit or be handicapped for a long time to come. If an employee is well-trained, his or her motivation and job satisfaction can receive a boost that later leads to many good things for the manager as well as the worker.

Office Education (as Distinguished from Training)

Untrained employees who also lack any basic "office education" present unique problems. Some people do not have any vocational education that has prepared them to serve in an office. Office education should make them qualified to perform some of the many techniques used in offices and improve skills they may already have.

An understanding of the *facilitating function* provided by an office such as yours would be very helpful to a new trainee. Your office, for example, undoubtedly provides many different facts to management. It assembles data. It simplifies and summarizes information. In short, it facilitates the work of a busy executive. If you feel that the recruit who has been hired (and is ready to be trained) does not have the educational background to understand these basic office functions, assign someone to escort the person on a walking tour around the office. A brief explanation of the work done by various departments would be enlightening. And the opportunity to watch office equipment in action could say more than many words of explanation.

What Is Training?

Possibly there is *no training program in your office*, even though you bring people aboard fairly regularly! While new employees undoubtedly learn things, they may not be getting trained according to the definition used here. Simply having an employee learn a job from someone else who is now doing it is not training. Training is not just "show and tell." Likewise, asking an employee to learn the job from a procedures manual, or from a machine operator's instruction book, is not training.

Here's what a formal training program involves. It is:

Formally organized
Assigned to someone as a responsibility
Preplanned as to content and approach
Controlled as to timing and results
Designed to achieve a prescribed level of performance

Good formal training programs have become increasingly important as office work has grown more complex and technical. In the office of tomorrow (to be discussed in the last chapter of this book), a well-conceived training program will be an absolute must.

Characteristics of a Good Training Program

The best way to ensure that training accomplishes what it should is to follow the principles that educators have established for developing vocational training programs in high school. These are as follows:

1. Set forth the training objectives. These should be formally stated, to be used as a guide by the trainer and trainee alike. Training objectives should cover the learner behavior after the training is completed and also the range of acceptable performance.
2. Analyze the job that is to be filled and break it down into components. The components should be taught in the same sequence as they are intended to be performed.
3. Train the trainer before expecting him or her to train the applicant. The trainer should know how to communicate as well as knowing the job characteristics.

4. Build the principle of feedback into the training, so that the trainee is able to learn how well he or she has performed *promptly* after job completion.
5. Recognize the principle of the learning curve, which means that the trainee gradually improves his or her performance after being on the job for a reasonable length of time.

Orientation as a Part of Training

Many office managers consider orientation to be a completely separate activity from training, whereas in actuality it is one of the most critical phases of the training program. During the first few days on the job, and while the new employee feels the most insecure, it is very beneficial to indoctrinate him or her about many phases of the work *that are not related to actual job performance*. To start a new employee off on the right foot:

1. Introduce fellow workers.
2. Show the workplace and explain technical features (if any).
3. Review working hours. Demonstrate use of the time clock (if any).
4. Show where restrooms, drinking fountain, and coat rack facilities are.
5. Explain lunch-hour and coffee-break rules.
6. Explain how and when regular salary is paid and standard policy regarding raises.
7. Outline the work of the office and how the employee will fit in.
8. Discuss various "fringes" and provide written pamphlets (if any).

Assessing Training Needs

Many employees—either those newly hired or those presently on the staff—should be given "customized" training. Systematic collection of data regarding necessary office tasks will reveal what work is to be performed and where, how, and by whom. Such requirements can then be matched against the capabilities of current office workers to establish training needs. These data are best collected by questionnaire, but if your group is small enough, other acceptable data-collection methods are to directly observe workers, hold group meetings, or obtain information from department supervisors. *What should be taught* is not always *what the employee wants to learn*. If the two don't match, your training dollars can be misspent.

Obtaining "Agreement" on Office Training Programs

Another factor to be considered is the office employee's receptivity to training. No training has any value unless it is acceptable to two parties—namely, the prospective learner and his or her boss. Of the two, it is much more important to deal with the learner, since he or she must (1) want to partake of the training, and (2) benefit from it. The method of obtaining such agreement from the learner is sometimes formalized through execution of an actual "learning contract." With a learning contract, the employee participates in the processes of diagnosing his training needs, formulating his objectives, identifying resources, choosing strategies, and then evaluating his accomplishments after the training is completed. In this manner, the learner develops a sense of ownership of and commitment to the planned instruction.

Learning contracts are valuable because adult learners often do not respond in a so-called "normal manner" to traditional teaching. For instance, when employees learn something "on their own" pertaining to their job (as contrasted with being told that they must have such training), they are highly self-directing. If an employee decides to learn on his own initiative, he would probably learn more deeply and permanently than in the office-sponsored training setting.

Of course, those kinds of learning that are engaged in purely for personal development are often planned and carried out completely by an individual on his own terms. By way of contrast, those kinds of learning *selected by your office*, which are designed to improve the employee's technical competence, must take into account the needs of both the office department where the employee works and the entire organization. Thus, your employee may feel that his or her personal needs are being subordinated. Learning contracts provide a means for negotiating a reconciliation between these "external" needs and expectations, and the individual's "internal" personal needs and interests.

Furthermore, with professional business seminars, the learning activity is structured by the instructor and perhaps also by your office. Thus, the prospective learner may be told by several authorities what objectives he is to work toward, what resources he is to use, and how and when he is to use them. This structure, which is imposed from the outside, may conflict with the employee's deep psychological need to be self-directing and may induce resistance, apathy, or withdrawal. Learning contracts provide a vehicle for making the planning of learning experiences *a mutual undertaking* between a learner and his boss, or between a learner and an outside instructor.

Finally, in management-oriented learning particularly, there is a strong possibility that *what is to be learned by individuals* will be less clear to both the learner and the boss than what *the "final outcome" is intended to be* for the whole group of office administrators. Learning contracts offer a means for making learning objectives clear and explicit, not only for the prospective learner but for his boss or bosses. This can be very beneficial to your office, since it causes all the bosses and all the learners to help set the learning objectives *together* and then to strive to achieve those objectives through a joint effort. Thus, you can obtain a greater assurance that the money spent for training will achieve the ultimate goal—better-trained and more competent personnel.

Many employees will not be accustomed to such a formal approach in a learning situation. In fact, some may consider the process of contracting to learn something as offensive, perhaps as an insult. This could indeed be the reaction, if the learners enter into such agreements solely because of coercion. However, if there is an opportunity for the prospective learner to "bargain" for the intended learning result, the reaction should be much different. In short, your employees are more likely to respond to training if they have participated in defining it than if training conditions are imposed on them by pressure from their immediate supervisor.

This may be a facet of office-work training that had not occurred to you. Before you dismiss it as too theoretical or impractical, stop and consider this. Sometimes, employee turnover, absenteeism, and low morale can be traced to inadequate or poorly designed training programs. This is in addition to the lower output, poor quality, and increased costs that are generally associated with inadequate training. Clearly, the nature of your work training programs can have a significant impact on office profitability.

Appraising the Performance of Trained Office Employees

There is probably no other process which is as difficult for office managers to perform correctly as the appraisal of their subordinates' performances. Perhaps managers are uneasy about "judging" someone, and thus are hesitant to criticize poor performance. Possibly their own biased outlook is clouding the appraisal process. Very likely, part of the problem is that so much office work is difficult to rate as to accuracy or adequacy. For these and various other reasons, performance appraisals are frequently poorly done in today's offices. This section is intended to help correct the situation, if it exists in your office.

Tools for Ranking Personnel According to Their Performance

There are a variety of devices available for rating employee performance. These range from the very simple to the complex.

Straight annual ranking. This is simply a procedure of comparing all of your employees' performances once each year, identifying the most superior person, identifying the next most superior one, and so on down to the worst performance.

Alternative ranking. This is a more complex approach to the same end. The evaluator is given a list of employees and selects only the best and the worst performers. These two employees are deleted from the original list and placed at the head and the foot of the ranking list. The evaluator next selects the best and the worst from the shortened list, and these, too, are deleted and transferred to the ranking list, and so on. The benefit of this approach is that the evaluator is required to establish only two rankings at a time—that is, the best and the worst—from an increasingly smaller original list.

Preestablished annual grouping. Once each year the evaluator places a designated portion of employees within preestablished categories. For example, the evaluator could be told to group employees in a particular department in the lowest 15 percent, the next 20 percent, the middle 30 percent, the higher 20 percent, and the highest 15 percent. The principal problem with this approach is that when the number of employees is very small, fractions of persons end up being assigned to each group.

Critical-incidents method. Specific activities (or "incidents") are selected that are essential to successful performance of each job in a department. Separate analyses of these are performed in every case, and a translation into behavioral categories is performed. Such things as thoroughness, accuracy, and promptness would be among the selected behaviors. The evaluator then makes a subjective comparison between the person assigned to the work and the ideal characteristics that are needed to get that job done.

Discrete rating scale. This approach is the most popular one, because it can be applied to a small group of employees and because it is easiest to carry out. Figure 4 illustrates a simply designed form. The evaluator uses a separate form for each employee and places an X mark in the appropriate place on the scale to indicate his or her rating of the employee in each category. The number of categories that are being mea-

Figure 4. Discrete rating scale of performance evaluation.

	Distinguished	Superior	Adequate	Below Average	Low
Attitude					
Volume of work performed					
Accuracy					
Overall Job performance					

sured could vary from the four shown in Figure 4 to as many as twenty different qualities. Obviously, the more categories there are, the more revealing the ratings will be to both the employee and the department supervisor.

Comparison with preestablished job evaluation. This more complex method is discussed at some length in Chapter 4.

Guidelines for Performance Evaluation

In the author's experience, no informal approach to rating can combine effectively with a formal system of performance appraisals. You must either be willing to require the supervisors of the several departments of your office to learn to conduct formal, one-on-one rating sessions with their subordinates, or be willing to do all the ratings yourself. In either case, there are some problems that you should be aware of. These relate to poor "people skills" on the part of the person doing the rating, and are as follows:

1. *Central tendency.* This is a tendency to consider all office employees as "average."
2. *Leniency.* Some people are unwilling to say something uncomplimentary or harsh about an employee, no matter how deserved such comments are.
3. *Over-criticalness.* This is the opposite of leniency; an inability to find anything commendable in the work performance of anyone.
4. *Procrastination.* Some people are inclined to put off rating for so long that it loses most of its relevance.

The above deficiencies can be avoided by adoption of a rating procedure with clear and positive rules. The following guidelines are suggested for your office:

• Performance evaluations should take place on a *regular basis*, certainly at least once a year. Scheduling every evaluation to coincide with an individual's birthday is a good idea, mostly because the department supervisor or the office manager doesn't have to deal with a heavy evaluation workload all at one time.

• *Behavior* (rather than personality) should be the only basis for performance evaluation. An employee can modify his or her behavior with practice and effort, but personalities are essentially unchangeable.

• Use a *"tell, then persuade"* technique when an employee is judged to be mature enough to avoid a defensive reaction. This is the most direct approach. The department supervisor or office manager simply tells the employee how he or she is performing and then persuades the employee to participate in developing a plan for overcoming problem behavior. Most people want to do a good job and keep the boss happy. Thus, this technique can be quite effective with stable employees who do not have too many fixed ideas or grievances about their work.

• Use a *"tell, then listen"* technique in all other cases. This approach involves telling the employee how his performance is perceived from the department supervisor's or office manager's perspective. Then the employee is asked how he feels about the evaluation. With this method, it is often difficult to avoid arguing with an employee who develops strong defensive feelings or who disagrees completely with the evaluation results. One of the prime purposes of any session pertaining to ratings is to encourage an employee to vent hostility or other negative reactions by "blowing off steam." Therefore, it is a mistake to try to suppress the employee's anger or prematurely to try to make him listen to reason (the boss's reason, of course). Avoidance of these behaviors involves considerable skill and self-control on the part of the department supervisor or office manager.

Some performance appraisers are sure to be far better than others at evaluating their workers. Those who have a natural empathy for people always do the best job. Also, it is easier to rate a person's performance when the individual responsible for the rating has a long period of acquaintance with the employee, and when mutual feelings of trust and tolerance have been established. A word of caution is in order at this point. No technique is perfect; no evaluation approach is without its flaws. The best you can hope for is to encourage individual employees' growth and improvement of their work performance.

Conclusion

This chapter has been designed to help you accomplish something very worthwhile yet also very difficult: to develop a staff of workers who will closely fit the expanding needs of your office and who satisfy work objectives with respect to both quantity of output and general abilities. Every office manager today faces a very difficult task when it comes to personnel administration. The diversity that exists in any business, the many fluctuations in work volume, the technical nature of much work, and the pressures of society all combine to make this job arduous. When the office is increasing in size and importance, still another dimension of difficulty is added. It is hardly likely that the future will bring a reversal of present trends. Office managers will need to be increasingly sophisticated and skillful in understanding worker behavior and learning how to modify it.

On the positive side, solution of personnel administration problems will impart more respect and authority to an office manager. The future looks very challenging but also quite promising for every office manager, such as yourself, who intends to be part of a growing and profitable organization.

3
Supervising Your Office Personnel

In the preceding chapter, the people who work in your office were considered in much the same way as the furniture—how many pieces of what kind are needed to get the job done. Now it's time to take a different focus. The business community has gradually come to accept the prime importance of "people factors" as they affect how well an office is run. Managers across the board generally understand the fact of individual personal differences, which often affect the ways in which various workers approach their jobs.

Despite these differences, many general statements can be made about that complex array of individuals who "people" today's offices—your growing office, for example. One basic similarity is the fact that *all* office workers change after they are hired and trained. They grow in knowledge, they become more skillful, they adopt new attitudes, and they develop additional expectations. It's up to you to see that your personnel change in ways that are positive and that enhance the productivity of the office. *Supervision* is the term customarily applied to all of the managerial processes that must be followed to influence these changes.

Are Office Workers Easy to Supervise?

At the outset, let's discuss a fairly common opinion. Many people, possibly including you, think that supervisory problems arise mostly in factories. After all, when you read or hear about labor troubles these days, it's always the miners or steelworkers or auto assemblers who get the headlines. So, since these industrial workers create all the agitation, they must be more difficult to deal with. Right? As with most easy solutions offered in this complicated world, to answer "yes" to the above question would be simple, straightforward, and wrong. The correct reply would be that office workers have *different* problems and thus require a *unique approach* to supervision. Just consider some of the variances between factory workers and office workers.

Working conditions. As you know, office employees don't have to deal with grease or dirt, and are seldom subjected to excessive noise. But office workers can become very militant about unsatisfactory working conditions. If you've ever shifted desks around, so that some people are closer to (or further away from) a window or an air conditioning outlet or the drinking fountain, you know all about that. Still, working conditions are generally better in offices than in factories, which makes for fewer supervisory problems.

Unionization. Many more factory workers are unionized than are office workers. Certainly, a small but growing office such as yours will be non-union. Therefore, your variety of supervision won't deal with uniform work situations that have originated among a large and homogeneous group. You must deal with individuals. That can be either good or bad, depending on circumstances. It certainly is different.

Closer proximity to top management. Many office workers are stationed in the same general area with the upper levels of management. They often see and sometimes converse with these high-level people. (In contrast, most factory workers have no contact at all with top management.) The problem with so much "togetherness" is that office workers may receive frequent reminders of great differences between their status and that of the "big shots." They see such people keep irregular hours, dress in an affluent way, and act important. Thus, there is much more potential for dissatisfaction among the office rank and file. The result—a more difficult supervisory task for you.

Jobs in transition. As described in the final chapter of this book, many technological changes are in store for offices in the next ten years. Possibly your office hasn't experienced many such changes, or perhaps the workers are just beginning to be touched by electronic data processing. Even where these advances haven't yet had much impact on office work, the staff will have heard enough about them to start to worry about their security. We are presently at the beginning of an especially difficult period for office supervisors. When people become concerned about something as fundamental as losing their jobs, other kinds of concerns are magnified as well. And who is the lucky person that everyone looks to for solutions? You guessed it—the office manager.

Predominance of female workers. A business office today is principally the domain of women. Nationally, more than two-thirds of all office workers are female, and that number is probably close to the proportion in your office. At the beginning of their employment, many women still anticipate that they will marry and don't expect to work for too many years. However, with the current high cost of living, an increasing number of women now see themselves punching the time clock for a long time, even after marriage. As a result, they are beginning to expect more from their jobs; they are becoming career-oriented.

For best results, supervisors must learn to deal somewhat differently with females in the office. (This applies whether you yourself are a man or a woman.) Your female employees may be undergoing substantial changes in outlook. They may be confused regarding proper attitudes and aspirations. It will be up to you to proceed carefully with these employees if you want to stimulate them to turn out a fair day's work, or to correct some undesirable situation.

Considering all of the foregoing changes, the responsibility for office supervision should be perceived as quite challenging. Let's begin to review the details of that responsibility.

Communication: The Heart of Office Supervision

The times when communication in the office is highlighted as being vitally important are those times when it has been poorly handled. If there is a work emergency or an office output foul-up, you can bet your next salary check that one of the deficiencies behind that problem was a lack of communication. Generally, the trouble was simply that Employee A had some important information and Employee B needed to know it, but, unfortunately, the information wasn't passed along. Or, if it was conveyed from A to B, it was either garbled or too late. In short, humanity in general—and very likely, both you and your office staff in particular—need to better understand the art of communication.

In the course of a typical workday, most people assigned to routine clerical jobs spend 10 to 15 percent of their time reading and approximately the same amount of time writing. A good part of the remainder of their day is devoted to speaking or listening. What is the reason for these latter activities? Simply the transfer of information. As business becomes more complex—and as organizations such as your office grow in size—more and more data must be exchanged. Accordingly, there is greater opportunity for erroneous transmissions to occur.

Furthermore, since you, personally, are charged with the duty of managing these people, you should be an exceptionally skilled communicator. When a boss conveys or receives information, he or she is often involved with the *exchange of ideas* rather than *transmission of facts*. Unfortunately, ideas (which may be abstract or inexact) are generally harder to explain and more difficult to understand than facts (which usually are definite and specific). When you issue instructions, or carry out any of the supervisory acts that come under the general heading of "exercising control," your communications are likely to be loaded with *qualitative* rather than quantitative terminology. You may use vague words such as "more" (more work, more efficiency, more income) or "less" (less cost, less delay, less downtime). Unless great care is taken, vague or subjective communications can be interpreted in various ways. Sometimes, the misunderstanding only has to do with the *degree* or *extent* of an instruction. The employee might be roughly aware of what you had in mind; he or she simply is unsure of how far to go in carrying out the instruction.

In short, then, supervisory communications are among the most difficult of all types to issue or receive. Yet, communicating is one of the most important duties that you have as an office manager.

Communication Feedback

In the author's consulting practice, when a boss habitually complains that he "can't get people to do what I tell them," this immediately signals the possibility that such a manager doesn't recognize the principle of feedback. He or she tends to think of any message as being one-way. In reality, the most efficient exchange of information between two people should be in the form of a loop, or two-way. (See Figure 5.) This principle applies to any attempt to convey information, but most specifically, it pertains to the messages that someone in authority must write or say, in order to get things done.

Figure 5 is simply explained. Person A (the sender) must share some information with Person B (the receiver). He or she transmits it either in writing or orally. While Person B is receiving the information, there may be interference. In a business office, the interference could be as simple as a noisy machine or the conversation of others. Other kinds of distraction could include work stress, undue emotion on the part of the receiver, fatigue, and so on. In any case, Person B knows that information has been transmitted, and believes that he or she understands what it is. However, to *ensure* that a true understanding has been reached, Person B should close the loop by restating the information in some way and "feeding" it back to Person A. Again, there may be outside interference.

Figure 5.   The communications loop.

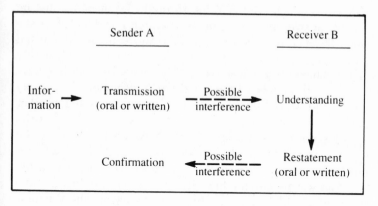

But Person A should try to make sure that what was sent back is the same information as he or she originally transmitted.

Certain office procedures include a communication loop as part of the normal routine. (That's the purpose of "acknowledgment," which is often requested to be returned after an order or some similar document has been processed.) But even when there is no standard way to close the loop, its a good idea either to repeat what someone has told you, or to ask the other party to say back what you have told him. An easy way to do this is to use some such phrase as "what I hear you saying is . . . ," whenever data are transmitted. Adopt this as one of your own work habits. Many times you'll be glad you did.

Communication Obstacles

Frequently, barriers get in the way of effective office communication. It's important for you to be aware of the variety of things that could go wrong.

There is often a problem *with the message itself*. The following incident, taken from the author's consulting practice, provides an example. An office manager wanted to make sure that some routine work had been completed. This manager decided to ask the head of the typing section about the work. Unfortunately, he didn't think through the question that he wanted answered by her; he approached her desk while she was talking on the phone. As soon as she hung up, he blurted out, "Sally, get me a list of the dates when those monthly maintenance reports were turned in." Note that he didn't say *what* month or *when* he needed the information. He simply turned and walked back to his office, without knowing whether the woman had understood him at all. Also, the head of the typing section hadn't originally done the work herself, so she had to inquire about it. What's more, the woman saw this incident as one in a string of occurrences she had been disliking. She was perceiving herself as often being reduced to the status of a "girl Friday" by this very manager who was now asking for information that she thought he should collect himself.

Several communication obstacles have been illustrated by this example. The first obstacle has to do with the *composition of the message*. The most efficient way to ensure that a message is a "good" one is to think about it before speaking or writing. Yet many people fail to do this. They consider it satisfactory to select some words relevant to the subject and instantly speak or dictate them. People like this "know what they want to say," so they use the first words that come to mind. This error sounds obvious. But if you were to list the basic steps of communication, would you list *preplanning the message* as Step 1? Perhaps not, but preplanning is the first important element in an effective exchange of information.

Even a message that is well composed and properly transmitted can fail to get through at the receiving end. A typical condition occurred in the example above—*how well did the head typist listen?* Remember, she had a preexisting bias against the office manager. Also, she had just finished another conversation on the phone and may still have been thinking about that. Further, she wasn't directly familiar with the work that the boss had asked about. Another consideration was how well her personal listening habits were established. That's one thing that we don't know from the example, but it is very important to think about.

Listening Skills

Listening is a skill that must be learned and then practiced regularly. Few people do it well. Many poor listeners are not aware that they have a problem. Most of us confuse *listening* with *hearing*. If we can hear someone who is telling us some information, we somehow feel that those voice sounds are all that we need to receive the message and retain it in our minds. Nothing could be more incorrect. When a listener simply hears someone speak, two major ingredients are missing: attention and empathy. Consider Figure 6, a diagram of effective listening steps. The first two sets of steps—physical action and mental effort—result in understanding of the message.

To achieve the listening skills that Figure 6 describes, try the following self-help measures:

1. Attempt to make the talker feel at ease. Assume a sympathetic facial expression.
2. Face the speaker directly. Act as interested as possible.
3. If there are outside distractions, either ignore them through concentration or move to a less distracting place.

Figure 6. Requirements for effective listening.

Physical Action	Mental Effort	Response
Step 1: Concentrate on the speaker (and)	Step 4: Interpret (and)	Respond verbally (and/or)
Step 2: Hear the message (and)	Step 5: Associate with other known facts (and)	React physically (and/or)
Step 3: Notice nonverbal communication signs	Step 6: Reach a conclusion	Retain mentally

4. Try to imagine the talker's situation. Put yourself in his or her place. In other words, empathize.
5. Allow enough time for the talker to say everything.
6. Ask leading questions.
7. If there are points you don't understand, say so and request more explanation.
8. Don't do any of the following:
   Criticize or argue
   Lose your temper
   Talk back too much

Motivation: The "Lever" for Good Office Performance

Many office jobs inherently lack those attractive qualities that generally appeal to workers and that contribute to high morale. Here are some common problems:

- The work may be monotonous and boring.
- Jobs are often so segmented that no worker carries the whole process through or sees the total picture.
- The results of the work are often intangible.
- The physical environment of the office may be uninteresting or confining.
- Little prestige may be associated with the work.
- In offices, pay and fringe benefits are generally lower than for factory jobs, especially for women.

In any of these situations, an office manager who wants to improve employee morale and motivation may feel that he or she has undertaken a very frustrating task. However, if workers can be persuaded that their jobs are important, and if the boss communicates overall objectives to the work crew and explains how such objectives will benefit the organization, office morale and motivation can be built and maintained at a reasonable level. The result of good morale—more work for the same pay.

The Desire of Office Employees to Be Closely Knit

In one of the most important studies ever made of human behavior in the workplace, a research group from the Harvard Business School found that every worker needs to conform and to feel secure within his or her group on the job. The researchers discovered that workers were unwilling to alienate their associates by surpassing them in workmanship. This means that competitive situations among office workers can lower job satisfaction and undermine morale. If you've ever considered using rivalry to increase accuracy or the quantity of office output—forget it. The only way to raise those standards is to stimulate everyone equally. Even under the most satisfactory working conditions, such as those provided by a plush office, morale can suffer if the environment is too "cold" and competitive. Most office staff members value a comfortable sense of belonging.

Personal Contact with the Office Manager

One of the problems with an office night crew may be a feeling of being left out, if the "big boss" (the office manager) never shows his or her face during the second shift. Particularly in a growing office such as yours, if only one to two people work at night, you ought to stay late at least once a month. When you are present, try to make every worker understand the importance of his or her job. This won't happen unless you communicate what the work objectives are and what progress is being made toward achievement of those objectives. Everyone needs to feel that he or she is contributing to the good of the company as a whole.

Naturally, the sense of being a part of the whole organization will differ from group to group. Sometimes a selected number of employees in an office suffer from *too much* personal contact. If those people get the feeling that someone is looking over their shoulders constantly, their motivation will decline sharply. Workers need to know that they are trusted;

morale will have a better chance to grow if the boss delegates equitably and extensively. So your separate work groups can either develop a stronger *esprit de corps* or not, depending on how much trust and recognition they get. You need to realize the value of simply giving experienced workers more responsibility and freedom. If they can't be let alone and trusted—get rid of them or move them to less responsible jobs.

Recognition of Worker Individuality

Some office managers still believe that employees work only for money, and that better work will automatically follow a raise or a bonus. Such managers may also try to use the issue of pay in a negative way: by threatening to cut wages or fire people in order to keep them on the ball.

The above tactics are effective to some extent, particularly in bad economic times, because everyone works to earn enough to buy the things he or she needs for self and family. Also, monetary awards have a certain prestige value, because the employee with higher pay assumes that his or her importance to the office is in keeping with the size of the paycheck received.

However, psychological studies have shown that most office employees are *not working for money only*. As discussed earlier, a feeling of belonging to a group is of great importance to office workers. Likewise, a worthwhile self-concept—an individual's understanding that he or she is a valuable member of the organization—is of great significance. Finally, an employee's motivations are also influenced by many secondary factors that differ among the group—age, marital status, education, health, personality, and so forth. For example, an accountant in his late twenties with a growing family and a mortgage would probably be primarily motivated by a need to fulfill his financial obligations. On the other hand, a secretary in her thirties, divorced and feeling she is in a dead-end job, might well be primarily motivated by an opportunity to switch to a more promising career path. Finally, an older worker whose children are grown and whose house is mortgage-free would probably be relatively unconcerned about money, at least in terms of upcoming salary increases. Instead, that person might desire mostly to continue to be needed by the organization in spite of his or her advancing years.

Another complication to keep in mind is that workers have both short-term and long-range motivations. For instance, suppose your secretary suddenly shows a great interest in earning more money, requesting to be paid for overtime work and discussing the possibility of promotion to a better-paying job. Before you decide that she is a money-hungry employee who will do anything for a buck, it would be a good idea to try to learn about her life circumstances. She may be starting to make payments on an expensive automobile, or trying to help a young relative finish school. Similarly, you might find that offering to reimburse an employee for college tuition payments will improve his or her morale level, but don't expect that it will work forever. In fact, that employee might have a long-range goal of earning a college degree and then leaving your office to start his or her own business.

Some offices encourage baseball or bowling competition, various social activities, travel clubs, and so on in an effort to tie employees more closely to the organization. The effectiveness of these efforts will vary, depending on the company and on individual employees. Many times, an office manager might not be sure what works and what doesn't, insofar as better motivation and morale are concerned. Since this entire matter is so complex, requiring intensive study along with professional advice, some managers have given up on trying special programs. They have decided to stick to the basic factors of recognition and fair treatment, along with a decent salary, as the best approach to improved motivation.

In summary, an office employee will be properly motivated and will have reasonably high morale when he understands the goals of the organization, feels he is striving to reach those goals, and has a measure of security within the working group. Fortunately, most employees are largely self-motivated. They want to do a good job, and thereby maintain their own self-respect. With such people, you have only to treat them as fairly as possible to gain their loyalty. When the office manager and the workers understand that they all have something to give, as well as something to ask for, the group can be said to be well motivated.

Administering Discipline and Handling Grievances

Office discipline represents the other side of the motivation coin. If office workers can't be motivated to perform more profitably, then they must be directed to do so through the use of disciplinary measures. Of course, everyone in any office is continually subject to mild forms of discipline. That's the only way to ensure order rather than chaos and to get the work done. For most people, noncoercive discipline, plus their own self-control, is sufficient to bring this about. It is the few *other* situations that we will now explore.

To set the record straight, the office manager should *not* try to fill the role of a parent, who spanks a misbehaving child or sends him to bed without his supper. In fact, an office manager who administers discipline while he is angry is simply not exercising enough self-discipline himself. Instead, all uses of discipline that involve a penalty should really be regarded as a form of training. Realistically, you can't completely remold the character and personality of a misbehaving worker. All you can reasonably expect is a fair day's work in exchange for a day's pay. In other words, you want the person who is out of line to get back in line and measure up to the standards of the rest of the group. Unless you adopt this positive attitude, you'll create resentment on the part not only of the offender but of everyone who witnesses any overly harsh imposition of discipline. Being an effective disciplinarian is probably one of the most difficult parts of an office manager's job, and if you don't do it well, one or more grievances may develop. We'll talk about grievance handling shortly. But first, how should discipline be enforced?

The Principle of the Red-Hot Stove

Most writers about work discipline make use of the example of a red-hot stove. Let's set one in the middle of your office as the symbol of a strict work rule or policy. The situation has the following characteristics:

- *Well recognized.* Everyone will see the stove and be aware of it, just as everyone should be aware of any fairly enforced office policy.
- *Impartiality.* Every worker who touches the stove gets burned. Anyone who breaks the rule must be disciplined.
- *Advance knowledge.* We all know that a red-hot stove should be avoided. The existence of the policy and the consequence of breaking the rule should be equally well known.
- *Prompt response.* Touching the stove brings about an immediate burn. Disciplinary action should be just as fast if the rule is broken.

The effectiveness of enforcing discipline in this way is widely recognized. Parents may follow a similar principle in disciplining a child for some infraction of a rule at home.

Why Employees Break Rules

In order to be an effective disciplinarian, you first need to understand why employees break rules.

- Some employees are simply maladjusted people who are lazy or dishonest or careless. These are the so-called "hard core," or those most difficult to move toward desirable work performance. Someone of this nature possibly shouldn't have been hired in the first place, and may eventually be subject to disciplinary discharge.
- Some employees are immature individuals who don't respond positively to tight controls. This applies especially to

younger workers, or those who have grown up in a permissive atmosphere. A person like this will usually modify his performance after an infraction or two, particularly if he is "treated like an adult." His failings should be discussed calmly and in a non-autocratic way.

• Some employees have personal problems that cause them to be distracted or inattentive or emotional. This can be a difficult situation for an office manager. Obviously, you can't solve their off-the-job worries; on the other hand, you can't ignore the fact that a problem exists. The best approach is to try to be understanding, yet to let such employees know that they must conform to the same rules that others are following, regardless of what is going on in their private lives.

• Some employees break rules in exasperation over what they regard as petty or senseless requirements imposed by an autocratic member of management. The author has encountered numerous instances of this in past consulting practice, and has coined the term "because I say so" rule to refer to such situations. Perhaps the most memorable example of this approach had to do with a door that employees were required to use when arriving for work or departing for home. A certain office, which shall be nameless, has two doors to the outside, on opposite sides of the building. Both doors are used by employees to go in and out all day. Neither can be locked after the building is opened for business, because other companies also use these doors. Yet, *because the office manager said so*, only one door adjacent to his office was to be used at starting and quitting time. The workers punched a time clock, so this arbitrary rule didn't serve the purpose of checking on promptness. In fact, there was no rational purpose for the restricting. However, the office manager referred to use of the other (forbidden) door as "sneaking in" or "sneaking out." If there are "because you say so" policies or rules in effect at your office, some of the more independent employees will occasionally break those rules purposely to express their defiance.

• Normally, many employees break rules as a result of ignorance, because they were distracted by some (possibly important) other event, or simply because of momentary forgetfulness. Earlier, it was stated that administration of discipline should properly be considered a form of training. If this attitude is taken, rule-breaking should diminish.

How to Be an Effective Disciplinarian

There are four simple steps involved when discipline must be administered.

1. *Find out exactly what happened.* When an office policy has been violated, there must be some form of evidence. Hearsay evidence is the weakest form of proof. Some written record is far better, but is seldom available unless the witness or witnesses always record such events promptly. So if you are notified that something has happened that goes against office policy, immediately instruct the person who has told you to put it in writing. If you, personally, see the event, make your own written record. And if the occurrence is at all serious, try to get at least two written statements.

2. *Promptly discuss the matter with the offender.* Promptly means before the end of the day, but after you have calmed down. The discussion should be held in private. Statements from the witnesses *in writing* should be used, instead of having those witnesses present. The offender's version should also be obtained, and compared with what others have said. If a serious penalty is involved, have the offender write, date, and sign his statement in your presence; then you countersign it.

Remember that you, in effect, are acting as prosecutor, judge, and jury in these matters. So be as lenient as possible, while still being fair to those other employees who *didn't* break the rule.

3. *Tell the offender what the standard penalty will be.* For every office rule, there should be an established penalty for breaking it. This includes even minor infractions such as poor deportment, coming to work late, and so on. If a behavior is bad enough to be prohibited, then it's sufficiently serious for you to decide on a penalty when you set up the prohibition. You should have a written record of what all penalties are to be, and it would also be worthwhile to post such a list for the

information of everyone concerned. Generally, to have any noticeable effect, penalties in the office are either time off without pay, or a written reprimand that is retained in the offender's personnel file. The penalty for accumulation of several such reports would be time off without pay and/or no merit increase at the next review time.

4. *Always retain the written reports.* To eliminate future disagreements and also to maintain accurate long-term records, it is imperative that every document relating to a particular incident be kept in a permanent file. Many office managers fail to perform this activity, presumably because it is too much trouble. However, the lack of reports such as this can handicap ongoing personnel administration. You never know when you'll need information about a past infraction, and no one's memory is perfect.

Warnings and Firings

Some offices include warnings as a part of the disciplinary process. Other offices employ warnings in lieu of any real action. In the latter case, a warning becomes a joke. In the former case, a warning will be understood as Step 1 in an increasingly severe set of penalties.

Firing can and should be part of the discipline process. It can be handled in one of two ways. First, an employee may be discharged as the last step in a series of increasingly severe disciplinary actions. Second, an employee may be discharged if he or she commits a single very serious offense. In such a case, you might want to consider the alternative of a supension of one or more weeks, followed by a probationary period. In other words, you should allow yourself more than one option. The following example will illustrate this point:

- You prohibit fighting in the office, and set the penalty as either discharge or supension.
- Several months later, two young male employees engage in what could either be very rough horseplay or fighting. You, personally, are out of the office at the time but your

secretary and another worker give you all the colorful details. Also, a wooden chair has been broken.

- Depending on your own interpretation, and also depending on the prior deportment and attendance record of these people, you could take any of the following actions:

  Fire one or both at once.

  Give one or both a two-week suspension without pay, plus six months of probation.

  Have them share the cost of replacing the chair.

Some offices have a plan that permits an employee to erase a written reprimand by a period of good behavior. Generally, this applies to reprimands for minor infractions such as poor attendance. The benefit of this feature is that the workers are more likely to feel that discipline in your office is considerate of special circumstances. For example, an employee might have a good reason for coming in late or leaving work a few minutes early.

The Value of a Formal Grievance Procedure

Just as you have certain expectations regarding employee performance and conduct, so will the workers in your office have some definite feelings of how they ought to be dealt with at work. If an employee has a complaint about the job, he or she is very likely to be less productive as long as that complaint remains unresolved. However, unless there is some established way for a situation like this to be brought out in the open and then corrected, the worker's output could be affected for a long time.

The author recently encountered the following situation: A particular office machine was so noisy that the machine operator was required to wear a hearing-protection device. When the office was rearranged, it was decided that the machine would be put in a small, separate room, in order to lower the noise level in the remainder of the office. However, the operator of the machine was neither consulted in advance nor informed of the reason for the move. She simply came to work on Monday, after the movers had been busy all weekend, and found out about her new work station. She took the change personally, feeling that the section leader was discriminating against her. However, she was a quiet person who was somewhat insecure, so she didn't express her feelings to anyone. Afterward, of course, her volume of work dropped noticeably.

This situation continued for almost eight months, until the office manager conducted his once-a-year discussion with this woman, on her birthday. Her low morale was easily corrected by an explanation and installation of a small window in one wall of the separate room. But how much better the employee would have felt *if a formal grievance procedure already had been established* in that particular office. The woman could have vented her emotions by filing a grievance, and the corrective measures could have been taken much sooner. The worker's lowered morale and the resulting reduced output would have been overcome three-quarters of a year earlier.

The Elements of a Formal Grievance Procedure

As stated earlier, this text assumes that your office is not unionized and, therefore, that no grievance method has been negotiated. Under these circumstances, you can easily establish a simple procedure for handling employee complaints. *Be sure to explain it carefully to the workers*, and to emphasize that it has been set up for their benefit. Then, also *be sure that it is always followed in the future*. The following practical steps are suggested:

Step 1. Each employee is permitted and, in fact, is encouraged to discuss every grievance with his or her immediate supervisor. The supervisor is told in no uncertain terms to try to solve each problem at that level, because if a solution isn't possible the employee can take Step 2.

Step 2. This step, if Step 1 is followed properly, is seldom necessary. The employee describes an unresolved grievance *in writing* and sends it *directly* to the office manager. The written complaint doesn't "go through channels" where it might get sidetracked. The office manager discusses the complaint with both the worker and the supervisor. It should be possible to solve 99 percent of all grievances right there. However, for those rare hard nuts that can't be cracked, the final step should be available.

Step 3. This step requires the prior appointment of a "grievance committee." If you decide to go that far, keep the committee small, have both lower ranks of supervision and several workers as members, and make sure that there are no radicals on the committee. (For best results, the author recommends that all persons appointed to the committee be mature, experienced employees.) The committee should always schedule a get-together once a year, and should also meet whenever a Step 2 grievance can't be solved. All committee meetings should be held on company time. Decisions should be reached by a majority vote. The members should review each unresolved grievance with the complaining worker and with the office manager, and their decision should be final *unless* an expenditure of more than $100 is required. In the latter case, the approval of a financial officer (the treasurer or the controller) should be obtained. If such approval is not forthcoming, the grievance must be considered to be unresolved.

Your Leadership in the Office

Note that every step discussed so far in this chapter involves you working with people. Our thesis, then, is that an office manager *can only bring about increased profitability by good leadership* of his or her employees. Thus, it is appropriate to end the chapter by examining the ways in which leadership can be exercised.

It is fairly easy to describe how to act as a leader. You decide what should be done. You get the workers to do it. It's that simple. But the $64 question is: What must be done to accomplish this? The reason such a question is so difficult to answer is that leadership qualities are very personal. The ability to lead is conditioned by the *whole personality* of the individual leader. In fact, some heavy thinkers on this subject refer to leadership as an "art." The implication is that some can lead but others can't, just as some can paint a picture or compose music but others can't. That's an oversimplification, as far as leadership is concerned, because it is possible to learn and to improve your ability to act as a leader.

Understanding Leadership Types

Very briefly, there are three basic ways for a leader to deal with other people—those who are supposed to "follow the leader."

1. *Participative leadership* involves continuous interaction between the boss and the workers. The boss draws the workers into the decision-making process, and gets them to participate in determining when and how to do the job. This form of leadership is quite difficult to accomplish and will only work if the work force is qualified and loyal.

2. *Autocratic leadership* simply means that the boss tells the workers to jump and they jump. Some people work best under this form of control; others hate it. If the boss has autocratic personality characteristics, this can be the most "natural" type of leadership, and the easiest to perform.

3. *Abdication leadership* means that the boss informs the workers as to what should be done and then lets them decide when and how to do it. Possibly, abdication by the boss cannot be characterized as leadership at all. In any case, this type of activity is inconsistent with the exercise of responsibility by the boss.

Improving Your Leadership Skills

When fulfilling the role of leader, most successful office managers find various occasions to be *either* an autocrat or a participant. The choice depends on what kind of work needs to be done, what type of people are assigned to do it, and how much time is available. In other words, you judge the situation and then decide how to act to accomplish the desired result.

For some people, it's quite easy to switch from one style to another. Others find this very unpleasant. But there is no question that it can be done. The more you practice—the more frequently you serve successfully as a leader—the better you become. Here are the qualities that you should cultivate in yourself, in order to enhance your overall leadership performance:

1. *Knowledge of the work.* There is nothing more ridiculous than a leader trying to get people to do something that he or she knows very little about. Try to learn most details of the work in your office.

2. *Self-confidence.* If you don't feel that you can lead—you can't. You need to believe in yourself. But there is a difference between being self-confident and being cocky or arrogant about your role as a leader.

3. *Good judgment.* As you know, this comes with experience and with continued application of common sense. We will both agree that you are intelligent—otherwise, you couldn't retain your present position. Do your best to act wisely. You'll make some mistakes, but each error can provide a valuable learning experience.

4. *Willingness to work hard.* Leadership is one of the most difficult aspects of management; it requires considerable energy and dedication. As office manager, you probably are working harder than the rank and file of office workers—but perhaps your subordinates don't know this. Therefore, you should work long, hard, *and visibly* to convince others of your zeal.

5. *Integrity.* If people don't have confidence in you as a person, they won't accept your leadership. You should not take advantage of your position and should show that you are willing to "get your hands dirty"—to do unpleasant tasks rather than directing someone else to do them.

Your Attitude Toward Followers

Every leader, of course, has followers. It's time to devote some attention to the way you think about the people whom you expect to act as followers—the workers in your office. This subject is particularly significant because, in the final analysis, the responsiveness of those followers provides the best gauge of your leadership skill.

In earlier times, managers had a relatively low opinion of the work force and tended to deal with workers accordingly. The so-called traditional approach to leadership (or "Theory X," as McGregor called it) is based on the following assumptions about those who do routine office work:

- People will avoid work whenever possible because they are basically lazy.
- People prefer to be directed, rather than taking any initiative. They aren't ambitious and don't want to be given any responsibility.
- To get people to work, it is necessary to control them closely. In fact, many must be threatened with punishment before they will make sufficient effort to produce.

This theory, which is the basis for the autocratic style of leadership, is essentially negative in its outlook. A more positive (and more modern) approach is based on current understandings of human nature. The following assumptions, which comprise so-called Theory Y, are made about workers:

- Work is a natural form of human activity.
- People normally like to work. They are perfectly willing to strive to achieve objectives, if conditions are right.
- People will not only accept the responsibility delegated to them; under proper leadership, they will actively seek to assume more responsibility.
- More people are fairly creative and ingenious, but modern business life does not stimulate these human qualities. As a result, many "routine" workers are unable to work up to the full extent of their abilities.

This theory is the foundation for the participative style of management. In the past year or so, a still more positive theory of leadership—Theory Z—has emerged. However, this latest theory is not relevant here because it encompasses the entire organization, starting with the president or chief executive officer and working down from there.

The above remarks about leading and following do not begin to exhaust the subject. In fact, we can't deal with the most important element, namely *you*. You are the indefinable ingredient. The interest you have, the amount of nurturing and cultivation that you are willing to expend—these things will greatly influence the kind of leadership you display as an office manager.

Conclusion

By this time, you should be able to regard the management of your office as a real opportunity to contribute to the profitability of the organization. The proper exercise of management techniques produces good information, which contributes to effective administration, which makes money. Since people are such an important element of the office "work equation," an office manager can only achieve his or her own profitability objectives by influencing the staff to take proper actions. That's what this chapter has been about. It has described most essentials of the supervisory job. It has dealt with the individuality of personnel and some ways to stimulate appropriate activities on their part. Finally, it has briefly explored the nature of leadership in an effort to increase your interest in that subject. That's about as far as the written word can go. The rest is up to you. In both the long and the short run, the quality of your interpersonal relations with the work force of your office will have considerable influence on your success as a manager.

4
Controlling the Output of Your Office

In terms of *profitability* of office operations, the subject of output control would probably rank near the top of any office manager's wish list. How nice it would be to improve and increase output by means of control measures. Yet, how perplexing it is to try to decide which control measures should be used.

This chapter should help to solve the riddle for you. We'll be concentrating on three major topics:

- The scheduling of individual units of office output, as well as smoothing variations in the work flow
- The dynamics of office output—that is, the arrangement of work for greatest efficiency of output
- How the compensation of office employees can be related to their output

By devoting attention to all three aspects of administration, a manager can convert an uncoordinated, disorganized "paper factory" into an efficient office, smoothly turning out the proper volume of useful data in a timely manner, and with few emergencies.

Types of Office Output That Are Incompatible with Control

Not every kind of work carried out in an office lends itself to the control measures that will be described in this chapter. The following kinds of output *ought not* to be included as candidates for control:

- Specialized kinds of work are not compatible with over-all control measures.
- Work of low volume, even though quite standard in nature, is not worth the trouble to control.
- Work performed in scattered locations (as distinguished from work done at a centralized site) may be too difficult to bring into any uniform control system.
- Work that includes many exceptional situations or unique methods of handling will probably be too individualized to try to control.
- Finally, work that can't be "quantified"—that is, counted or measured through some uniform method—shouldn't be included in any control system, simply because you will never know how much work has been turned out. Thus, you can't judge the effectiveness of the controls.

Of course, with these limitations, much work in your office will remain outside the areas of control that this chapter describes. However, control can be exercised in other areas. High-volume work is normally where most of the expense and the headaches originate. So we'll concentrate on that kind of output in the pages which follow.

Planning for Better Work Efficiency

Planning is one of the basic functions of all types of management. Reduced to its simplest terms, planning involves a study of past events or situations and a projection of possible occurrences in the future. Sounds very high-toned, doesn't it? But realistically, we all plan. We may not call it by that name, but every person alive who wants to change his or her situation either acts on impulse or plans a course of action aimed at achieving a desired objective. It is hoped that as an office manager, you consciously decide to do some planning. But even if you don't set out to make a plan, you often do it anyway, simply by choosing between alternatives or by deciding the best way to proceed from Point A to Point B.

When it comes to planning for better performance of work, an office manager would first need to be aware of some possible improvements; planning how to achieve these improvements could then follow. In developing such a plan, here are some key questions that you might want to answer:

- What steps must be taken to fulfill the plan?
- When should each of these steps be completed?
- Are some of the steps interrelated? If so, what is the proper sequence for their performance?
- Will any established procedures be affected? If so, which procedures are involved and what would be changed?
- Will any present personnel be involved? If so, who are they and how will the change affect them?
- Will any new personnel be needed? If so, how many and what occupational types?

From the above, it is obvious that planning is no simple measure, to be taken lightly. Actually, *planning is a process*. It takes time, but it makes things happen. Planning reduces the chaos that we all experience from time to time when a serious, unexpected problem occurs. However, it is difficult to plan well, and a poor plan is not much better than no plan at all.

One important type of planning is the *scheduling of work performance*. Basically, work scheduling always requires a plan. The plan addresses the question *when*? Or, to be more specific, when should a given unit of work be started? Theoretically, work could simply be started as soon as the need originates, and that is the way that some offices try to deal with every job. But several factors will make such an approach undesirable, at least part of the time:

1. If some work must be expedited, while other work can be routinely handled, then a scheduling plan is very helpful.
2. If all or part of the office becomes overloaded with work, scheduling quickly becomes a paramount need.
3. If particular kinds of work are needed, but with required completion set far in the future, the work is likely to be forgotten unless it is "advance scheduled."
4. If the volume of work fluctuates widely, there are only two possible alternatives:
   Hire enough staff to meet demands, with the understanding that some people will be idle part of the time.
   Establish a work-scheduling system.

In real life, office managers don't wake up some morning and decide that henceforth, all work in their office is going to be scheduled. Instead, in most cases, an office manager is forced to begin a scheduling system because work is frequently overdue, priority commitments are not being met, and so on. Careful analysis of typical situations then generally reveals that either the office is overloaded or the volume of work is fluctuating a great deal (Conditions 2 and 4 in the foregoing list). As a consequence, the office manager may reluctantly decide that work scheduling will have to be carried out in the future.

However, a few office managers of the author's acquaintance are "presold" on scheduling. In fact, one of them holds a meeting with all of his key subordinates each week; the name of that particular gathering is the "when meeting." Each person who attends the meeting is expected to come with timetables for every rush job or unusual situation that is currently being handled in his or her section. By comparing and merging these timetables, the office manager can frequently determine an immediate way to resolve an emergency rather than having the emergency passed on to the next group assigned to process the work.

In view of the kinds of pressure experienced in many growing offices, it is a mistake to tolerate projects or jobs that are not sharply "when-focused." By establishing attainable time schedules and insisting that the schedules be met unless some real emergency prevents this, you can give the entire office the luxury of avoiding many last-minute crises. So, how can you set up a system that is "when-specific" for every high-volume job in the office?

Scheduling Office Output

High-volume office work is akin to the sort of factory work that is characterized by an assembly-line approach to output. It can and should be seriously considered as a subject for scheduling.

The Scheduling Chain of Events

A scheduling starting date must be established by working back from the due date of the specific job in question. This is considerably more than a simple mathematical exercise. For example, the *current workload* must be taken into account for each section that will handle the work. Also, the *total capacity* of the *people* and the *equipment* will have to be known in advance, and you will need to know *what volume* the new work will add to that which is already in progress. Finally, *prerouting* must be carefully thought out, so that the proper work path through the office section (or sections) can be selected ahead of time for each job.

Informal Work Scheduling

The simplest approach to scheduling of office work is to apply the familiar principle of "management by exception." When this method is utilized, *only rush jobs are scheduled*. It is assumed that the office is staffed to handle a constant flow of work, and such work will normally take a preestablished amount of time to pass all the way through the system. If a job must be given priority attention, then it is "traced" through every step of the work path, so that its rate of progress and current location are known at all times. If the job falls behind schedule, an "expediter" investigates the reason for the delay, tries to break the logjam, and then warns operations downstream that a priority job is coming through which is behind schedule. It is up to those downstream operations to help make up for the time already lost.

This so-called "informal" approach is the system to which the author generally gives first consideration, because it requires:

- A minimum of record-keeping
- The least possible personal attention from those who have the scheduling responsibility
- No involvement at all with the bulk of the work, which stays outside the expediting system

Unfortunately, when an *irregular work flow* is encountered, this informal system usually breaks down. Sometimes the work is very light and employees just can't find enough to do. At other times, the work is quite heavy and it begins to back up at every station. Then, even with the use of overtime, some of the regular jobs are delayed for several days. If there is a further sudden surge of work received, more jobs might be converted to the priority category. Suddenly everything could become a "rush job." If this type of situation continues for prolonged periods, the above-described informal scheduling system becomes no system at all.

The hypothetical example illustrated in Table 1 represents a single week of irregular work flow. On the basis of the information in this example alone, no one can say whether a situation is beginning that couldn't be effectively accommodated by the informal approach. A study of Table 1 leads to several conclusions:

1. The work volume was much heavier at the beginning of the week. Possibly, that situation is due to accumula-

Table 1. Variable office work flow.

			Hours Needed			
Day	Units of Work Received	Work Units, Output per Hour	Regular Work Time	Unused Time	Overtime	Total Actual Time
Monday	55	2.5	16	—	6	22
Tuesday	45	2.5	16	—	2	18
Wednesday	20	2.5	16	8	—	8
Thursday	10	2.5	16	12	—	4
Friday	15	2.5	16	10	—	6

tions of mail over the weekend. However, it could also
be a normal weekly cycle.
2. Two employees working 8 hours apiece can't handle the
work without overtime on Mondays and Tuesdays.
During the last 3 days of the week, one person could
handle the job alone and still have 6 hours left over (4
hours unused time on Thursday and 2 hours on Friday).
3. There is an apparent policy that all work must be completed on the day received. If this were changed to permit some work to be held over until the following day,
all overtime could be eliminated.

The purpose of the preceding example was to illustrate
how office policy can affect scheduling activity. If the permis-
sible processing time were changed (as suggested in Point 3
above), there would be *no informal scheduling needed.* The
changed example shown in Table 2 reflects that new situation.

Our two examples, taken together, are intended to indicate
the potential for an office to become overstaffed when there
are wide fluctuations in the volume of work, and *when the
management has no way to keep track of backlogged work.*
You might imagine the supervisor of an office, where the illustrated work situation occurred, saying to himself, "Wow—I
saved 8 hours of overtime cost by changing that policy." Yet he
could also say, "Darn—I still have 22 hours of unused time
after changing that policy." Clearly any attempt at profitable
office management is at the mercy of unanticipated events, in
a situation like this.

Also, these two examples are very unrealistic in several
respects:

- It would be remarkable if every work unit were to take
exactly the same amount of time (i.e., 2.5 units can be
completed every hour). Even when routinized work is
involved, there are minor variations from time to time,
which modify the needed time per unit.
- The examples do not make allowance for unusual re-
quests to expedite, which might occur at any time and

Table 2. Variable office work flow—modified.

Day	Units of Work Received	Units of Work Completed	Units Carried Over to Next Day	Work Units, Output per Hour	Hours Needed		
					Regular Work Time	Unused Time	Total Actual Time
Monday	55	40	15	2.5	16	—	16
Tuesday	45	40	20	2.5	16	—	16
Wednesday	20	40	—	2.5	16	—	16
Thursday	10	10	—	2.5	16	12	4
Friday	15	15	—	2.5	16	10	6

which could then call for rearrangement of some completion dates.
- In addition, a constant work force and uniform availability of equipment are assumed to be on hand at all times. Most office managers would be tempted to use some colorful language in commenting on the likelihood that this would always be the case.

With the possible deficiencies of an informal scheduling system so clearly set forth, you might be wondering if there isn't a better way. And there is!

Formal Work Scheduling

Formal work scheduling is a system that your office can really take advantage of, so long as two prerequisites are met.

- You must be willing to input information for every batch of work as it progresses through the office.
- A small office computer must be available for part-time scheduling use. (The versatility of a small computer will be discussed in Chapter 8.)

You may recall that back in Chapter 2, there was considerable discussion about estimation of the work hours needed to accomplish different office objectives. If your office workload is large enough to justify a computerized scheduling system, such a system not only will provide a running record of work in progress but can give you even better estimates of work-hour requirements *as a by-product*.

In order to introduce this more elaborate concept, you'll need to develop some fairly detailed records and procedures.

- The high-volume types of work in your office must be broken down into separate operations (or "jobs").
- The time required to complete a single unit of each operation must be realistically estimated. The total of estimates for all operations will then equal the time needed

for one unit of the work to be processed from beginning to end.
- A starting point must be established, where units of high-volume work can be detected and logged into the system. Another point must be established where the work officially ends, and where units can be logged out.
- A method must be set up for recording movement of the work from one operation to the next.

Besides developing detailed records and procedures, you must design (with the help of your friendly computer programmer/analyst) a series of computer programs that will accomplish a variety of things. The system must permit new units of work to be added to the schedule *as soon as they are received* (rather than when work on the first operation is started). This will produce an accumulating total of backlogged work (on hand but not yet begun) for each separate operation, which will fluctuate depending on how much comes in and how much of each operation is completed. Then, as a unit of work is actually started, and as it moves from one operation (job) to the next, "move" tickets will need to be prepared and recorded. The processing of these tickets will have a dual result: (1) the schedule itself will reflect the current location of all units of work; (2) the backlog record for each operation will show how much work is on hand but not yet begun. Finally, a series of informative printouts must be developed, so that all of these data, contained within the computer, can be displayed for your benefit and that of your several section supervisors.

When such a system is up and running, you won't have to guess about the workers or equipment needed. You can obtain assurance that all units of work are flowing through the office, or, if such is not the case, the identity and location of behind-schedule work can be easily determined. With the help of the "graphics" capability of your computer, you can even produce graphs or charts to show a history of what has happened in the past and a projection of what is likely in the future.

The potential uses of this formal scheduling system can be more completely understood through a careful examination of Table 3.

Table 3. An example of formal scheduling.

PHASE 1

Two work units received but no operations have begun.

Work Unit #	Operation Letter	Est. Hrs. Req.	Work Backlogged			Work in Progress			Work Completed		
			A	B	C	A	B	C	A	B	C
1	A	0.5	+0.5								
	B	1.5		+1.5							
	C	3.0			+3.0						
2	A	0.7	+0.7								
	C	1.3			+1.3						
Totals			1.2	1.5	4.3	0.0	0.0	0.0	0.0	0.0	0.0

Table continues on the next two pages.

Table 3, continued.

PHASE 2

Another work unit received. Work has started on Operation A of the first two work units received in Phase 1.

Work Unit #	Operation Letter	Est. Hrs. Req.	Work Backlogged			Work in Progress			Work Completed		
			A	B	C	A	B	C	A	B	C
Opening Balance			1.2	1.5	4.3	0.0	0.0	0.0	0.0	0.0	0.0
1	A	0.5	−0.5			+0.5					
	B	1.5									
	C	3.0									
2	A	0.7	−0.7			+0.7					
	C	1.3									
3	A	1.0	+1.0								
	B	1.2		1.2							
	C	1.8			1.8						
Totals			1.0	2.7	6.1	1.2	0.0	0.0	0.0	0.0	0.0

Table 3, continued.

PHASE 3

Still another work unit received. The first two work units are now well along, and work has started on Work Unit 3.

Work Unit #	Opera-tion Letter	Est. Hrs. Req.	Work Backlogged			Work in Progress			Work Completed		
			A	B	C	A	B	C	A	B	C
Opening Balance			1.0	2.7	6.1	1.2	0.0	0.0	0.0	0.0	0.0
1	A	0.5									
	B	1.5		−1.5		−0.5	+1.5		+0.5		
	C	3.0									
2	A	0.7				−0.7			+0.7		
	C	1.3			−1.3			+1.3			
3	A	1.0	−1.0			+1.0					
	B	1.2									
	C	1.8									
4	A	4.0	+4.0								
	B	5.5		+5.5							
Totals			4.0	6.7	4.8	1.0	1.5	1.3	1.2	0.0	0.0

Scheduling Accompaniments

If you decide to accept the author's recommendation and convert to *planned* scheduling of high-volume office work, there are several other refinements which should be considered along with such a conversion. Since you'll be attempting to gain a more organized approach to output control, you'll need to review all the practices in your office that influence whether that goal is achieved.

Possible Causes of Work-Volume Fluctuations

Wide variations in the quantity of office work received represent a threat to every element of managerial control. You never know what to expect when the work doesn't flow in steadily. There may be problems with work assignments and the most efficient use of equipment. Previous planning or decision-making can be upset. Last but not least, work scheduling becomes more complex, as we have already discussed.

For all of the above reasons, it's worthwhile to briefly review the conditions of work-volume fluctuation, to mention some of the reasons why these fluctuations occur, and to suggest some countermeasures. Let's begin by itemizing some of the more common causes. Test these against working conditions in your office.

- Seasonal variations may sometimes occur in the activities of your company. Even though there is a time lag in record-keeping, these variations will sooner or later be reflected in a variable workload in the office.
- Sometimes, company policies "artificially" create fluctuations in office work-volume, by requiring certain record-keeping to be done at prescribed times.
- Every office experiences gaps in the work flow, brought about by personnel absences due to vacations, long weekends, or extended holidays.
- Breakdowns of equipment or unplanned absences of personnel create unexpected disruptions of work from time to time.

- Significant changes in procedures or in the way personnel are assigned to various jobs will interrupt work flow.

Administrative Remedies For Fluctuating Workloads

Some of the easiest (and most obvious) solutions to the fluctuation problem fall within your personal area of authority. Or, the solution might come under the jurisdiction of one of your peers in the organization. Here are some examples:

1. *Modifying policies.* In most offices, the payroll section must make periodic salary adjustments and earning computations, prior to the time that the payroll is written. With a semimonthly payroll cycle, this can mean a fairly light period followed by a few days of intense activity. However, if an administrative decision can be made to split the employees into two sections for payroll purposes, and to pay them on alternate weeks, the earning-computations workload becomes almost level.

2. *Adjusting deadlines.* In a sales office, where records are made of monthly selling activity by individual salesmen, it is common for the salesmen to avoid turning in their orders until almost the end of the month. This has the dual advantage, from the salesmen's point of view, of creating a "big splash" and also of concealing progress from the other, rival salesmen. However, from a clerical point of view, this practice creates a "famine," then too much of a "feast" of work. A simple solution, when different kinds of products are sold, would be to set up staggered month-end dates for those different product lines. In that way, every week of the month could be the final deadline for 25 percent of the company's product line.

3. *"Cycling."* Most banks, department stores, insurance companies, public utilities, and so forth have divided the letters of the alphabet into four discrete groups. Customers whose last name starts with the letter A (Adams, for example) receive their monthly bill during the first week of the month. Those whose last name starts with G, (Graves, for example) will receive their bill during the second week, and so on. If you have a large number of individual customers, you might want to set up two or more separate monthly cycles for billing them.

4. *Controlling backlog.* In those offices where the mail volume is full of peaks and valleys, the incoming mail could be held for a day or two in a "backlogged" status. Each morning, management would release only the amount of work that is possible to process in a day's time.

5. *Taking miscellaneous measures.* Prearranged fill-in work is a common office feature, during slack periods. Partial completion of work in advance of need is also a popular remedy.

Use of an Incentive System

Sometimes there will be a financial advantage in completing a certain type of work, no matter how much of it has been received in total. An example would be an insurance office, where work on processing the record of a new policyholder must be completed within a day or two, in order to get it on the books as soon as possible. Employees can be stimulated to work faster through use of a bonus or some other type of a prize for above-average output.

Overtime or Part-Time Help

If worst comes to worst, an office manager may have to resort to the use of overtime work or employment of part-time help to chip away at the mountain of work that sometimes piles up. However, this practice adds to clerical cost, and therefore deserves your special attention. Unless you are able to find some other solution (such as one of those explained above), the profitability of the operation will be affected.

Preplanned Dispatching and Routing of Output

After office work is accurately scheduled and then correctly timed, release of work units becomes an essential part of the system. Likewise, a standardized route from one operation to the next must be carefully worked out. The first step consists of proper batching of the work, prior to sending it on its way. Some work is "self-batching," in that different work units can't be readily merged. Other, more uniform types of work need to be arbitrarily collected into efficient batches, before being released.

Organizing the Office Work Flow

The "patterns" by which work processing is arranged in your office will have a considerable influence on the efficiency of that work. (As before, we are referring principally to large-volume jobs.) Just as the design of a factory assembly line can create either very effective or very cumbersome productive facilities, so the *organization of discrete steps* in performing office work can be crucial from the standpoint of profitability. This could be particularly true for an expanding office such as yours, where once-satisfactory arrangements could gradually be outgrown and therefore become obsolete.

Parallel (or "Vertical") Arrangement

Under this approach, which is the type favored by many small offices, the work is divided between groups or teams, with each team doing the same work as the others, and with *every team handling all the steps* from start to finish of the work. Usually, this means that each employee on the team can perform all necessary operations. Such a work arrangement is diagrammed in Figure 7. Note that this type of arrangement is compatible with *generalized* work training.

With this plan, it is possible to assign a wider variety of work steps than with either of the other two arrangements that will be discussed. Work can be handled more expeditiously because it is started and finished within a small area of the office—the workplace of the team—rather than being shifted from one section to another. On the other hand, it takes longer for an employee to learn the complete range of job steps. Also, since they have wider knowledge, persons performing the job may qualify for a higher salary. (This will be examined later in the chapter.) There is usually greater job satisfaction asso-

Figure   7.   Parallel work arrangement.

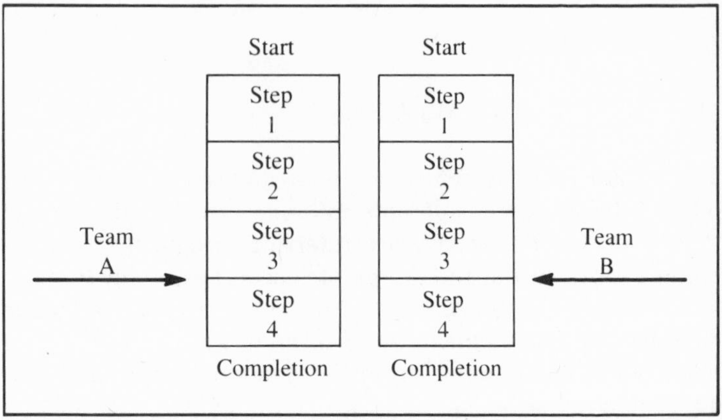

ciated with parallel types of work, because the jobs are more varied and interesting.

Serial (or "Horizontal") Arrangement

Under this approach, a unit of work moves through a series of desks or work stations, where different employees carry out various specialized operations. In such a setup, a number of individuals handle the work and no one employee is trained to do what the others can do. A sample serial arrangement is diagrammed in Figure 8. Note that this type of arrangement is compatible with *specialized* work training.

With this plan, employees are assigned to a single operation or only a few operations. Thus, the training time is relatively short and a minimum level of skill is required. Moreover, since the operations are usually fairly easy, employees of lower pay grades can be used.

However, it must be realized that, on special occasions, a much more skillful (and better paid) employee, such as a machine operator, is likely to be included in a serial work arrangement. For example, Step 3 in Figure 8 might be to enter certain data on a machine. This step would be performed by

Figure 8. Serial work arrangement.

Step 1	Step 2	Step 3	Step 4
Employee A	Team B	Employee D	Employee E

an accounting machine operator. Step 1 might consist of merely opening envelopes and extracting the contents. This part-time work could be performed by the receptionist or some other employee whose time isn't fully occupied. Step 2 could be performed by a team of data-preparation clerks, who might simply underline pertinent data that appear on the documents received in the mail. Perhaps these clerks could also perform a simple look-up job such as finding code numbers and entering one on each document. The entire purpose of this step might be to prepare the document for machine entry. After the machine operator completes the work during Step 3, Step 4 could simply consist of filing the document among a batch of other material that "went through the machine" on a given day. This simple job could easily be performed by a file clerk.

This scenario is not as entirely advantageous as it sounds. Since the work would move from one person's work station to that of another, there could actually be more handling of paper and more time required than the explanation above would indicate. Also, the end result of the process might be known only to the machine operator. Therefore, workers performing the monotonous Steps 1, 2 and 4 could not "see the big picture" and probably would feel very little job satisfaction.

Unit-Assembly (or "Simultaneous Work") Arrangement

This plan can only be utilized in special cases, where one unit of work can be processed *separately but simultaneously* by different work stations. For example, if a multiple-part customer order form were sent in by a salesman, one copy could be used to check the customer's credit rating, another copy could serve as an accounting document to support the entry that reduces the inventory for the material being ordered, and a third copy could act as the sales record. These three processing activities could take place at about the same time, after the mail was opened and the copies were separated and routed. Figure 9 illustrates the unit-assembly arrangement.

Obviously this is a highly unique kind of work arrangement. It cannot be directly compared with either the parallel or the serial arrangements described above. At the same time, it is certainly to be recommended as an effective form of work organization in those particular cases where it is applicable.

Considerations in Choosing Among the Three Arrangements

Very likely, your office has areas of high-volume activity where each of the above processing plans could ideally be installed. Most office managers find that the organization of all major clerical activities should be reviewed every year or so to detect inefficient arrangements. Here are some points for you to ponder:

Figure 9.   Unit-assembly arrangement.

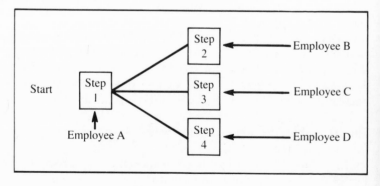

- Work that fluctuates widely in volume is not well suited to the parallel arrangement.
- The serial arrangement provides for the greatest economy in the use of scarce skills and equipment.
- The unit-assembly arrangement will take the least time from start to completion, since several steps can take place simultaneously.
- Under the parallel arrangement, it is easiest to establish responsibility for worker accuracy.

As is so often the case, you will probably be forced to balance one "good" against another, if you try to decide which work arrangement is preferable in given circumstances. For example, if speed of processing is considered to be of paramount importance, the unit-assembly arrangement should be seriously considered. If accurate output is more desirable than speed, the parallel form of work organization might be better. If worker morale has become a problem, possibly the serial arrangement of work is a contributing factor. On the other hand, if you must train a large group to perform complicated processing, then the serial arrangement is your best bet.

Office Compensation Related to Output

Generally, office managers find that the total of all salaries (plus fringe benefits) represents by far the largest single increment of expense in their office. As a result, when considering the subject of output efficiency, a major share of attention should be focused on *what functions* employees are paid to perform and *how much money* they receive. The profitability of office operations will depend to a considerable extent on *job-related employee compensation*. At the same time, it is always important (and sometimes difficult) to decide whether a particular employee should be "fitted" to a job or whether the job should be adapted to that employee.

In an expanding office such as yours, where technical knowledge and skill are required to perform many jobs, there may be a need for some "scientific" method of ensuring compatibility between the characteristics of the work and personal abilities. Such an approach could also help to make sure that people do what they're paid for. Descriptions of a model system of compensation, featuring a so-called scientific method of control, will occupy the remainder of this chapter. Six discrete steps have been developed, and are described below for your consideration:

- Analyze every job, following a standard analysis procedure.
- Write separate job descriptions, covering a prescribed scope of work factors, as contained in the job analysis.
- Evaluate each job in order to establish its relative worth to the office, using the job description as a guide.
- Use the above tools for periodic appraisals of how individual employees are performing on the job.
- Compensate the employees in accordance with their appraisal ratings.
- When appropriate, reassign personnel to different jobs, using other job descriptions and evaluations to help make the best selection.

Before you decide against the "luxury" of going through all of those steps just so that Geraldine's paycheck can be written, stop to consider what that paycheck could represent. To Geraldine, her pay, of course, means money for groceries and the rent. But it also ought to signify that she is recognized as a reliable employee, doing responsible work for a good company. If the paycheck is too low, Geraldine may feel hopeless or cheated. As she harbors resentment, she may become uncooperative and her work will suffer. The same amount will come out of the company's bank account, in either case. The point is that compensation should never be overlooked as a major factor contributing either negatively or positively to productivity.

A fair and equitable compensation system is directly related to the *most profitable use of payroll dollars*. Let's consider the details of the suggested system.

Job Analysis

Almost every office employee performs more than one activity. A receptionist may greet visitors, answer the telephone, sort the mail, and carry out other miscellaneous clerical functions. A machine operator may run the machine, fill out a log sheet, and sort or distribute documents. Furthermore, there is always a frequency, or number of times performed, associated with each separate activity. Finally, office jobs aren't static. New activities are added, other activities are discontinued. The frequency may change from twice a week to once a day, and so on. All of these dynamic aspects of office jobs must be reflected in the job analysis.

There are a variety of ways to collect and analyze data pertaining to office job features:

1. Workers may be interviewed by an analyst and asked to describe what they do. The various functions which the worker itemizes are then "located" in the *Dictionary of Occupational Titles*, published by the U.S. government. This approach helps to identify commonalities among jobs, which is very helpful when job evaluations are performed.

2. Workers may be interviewed and asked to describe activities considered critical to good or bad performance. Only these "critical incidents" are included in the job analysis. This method is particularly useful when employee performance is appraised.

3. Each worker may be asked to fill out a questionnaire (rather than being interviewed). A standardized questionnaire can easily be designed to fit the needs of your office and to build a "profile" for each job.

Job Descriptions

Each job description must be related to the content of the work. A number of key characteristics become important:

Contacts with customers or other "outsiders"
Kinds of prior knowledge or experience needed

Major job responsibilities
Important relationships with other jobs

These characteristics should be described in outline form, with standard phrases used wherever possible. It is best to give only one person the responsibility for writing all job descriptions, because consistency is very important. Of course, all descriptions should be reviewed by the immediate supervisors before they are accepted as "official."

Job Evaluation

There are three separate approaches to job evaluation. Each is in common use; choice of an approach depends, to a large degree, on the size of the office.

The "simple ranking" method. Under this approach, jobs are evaluated as a whole. A job's importance and value to the office are established by comparing its job description with descriptions of others that are considered similar. The result of this approach is a ranked list of jobs. This method is quite old. It had been in use for years before the author employed it one summer, while still in college during World War II. If your office has fewer than fifty different jobs, this method can work quite well, and the ratings are relatively easy to justify— provided the person doing the rating is a knowledgeable, unbiased member of management whose judgment is sound.

The "classification ranking" method. This method is identical with the simple ranking method explained above, except that all job descriptions are first arranged into classes (or groups), and then those classes are sorted in order of importance. This ranking technique still depends on subjective judgments, but the method is superior because related jobs *are considered together.* All secretaries, for example, no matter where located in the office and regardless of the different features of their jobs, would have their individual job descriptions classified and then evaluated as a "family" of secretarial positions. This method is recommended for offices of up to a hundred employees, with fifty to seventy-five different jobs.

The "quantified ranking" method. This approach features a plan of assigning either dollar values or points to a variety of different job characteristics. The approach is both technical and complicated. Usually, a trained evaluator should do the work. It is unlikely that your office will be large enough to justify this method. If it *is* that large, you'll need to thoroughly study the possibilities and problems involved. Since a few paragraphs of explanation won't provide enough information, we won't delve into the subject any further.

Performance Review

Performance appraisals were discussed at some length in Chapter 2. When performance review is built into the compensation system, it should serve three basic purposes: (1) promote the development of job skills; (2) pinpoint cases where more training is needed; (3) allocate monetary rewards. As you are undoubtedly aware, employee performance is an elusive and changeable characteristic. To attempt to appraise it is somewhat like trying to describe a Pacific sunset—mere words will fail you. Therefore, you'll need to establish a procedure and (unfortunately) a review form. Figure 10 should give you some ideas in this regard. Other methods of performance appraisal were discussed in Chapter 2.

You'll find that the most difficult problem with a performance review will be justifying a low rating to an employee. Most persons will ask to be given examples of their unsatisfactory performance. They will want to be told specifically what needs improvement. (Also, it's helpful to be able to say what, if anything, they've done that is commendable.) If the overall review rating is so far below the acceptable level that their compensation will probably be adversely affected, such an employee will very likely be defensive, and possibly will become emotional.

With such a strong reaction as a prospect, the fundamentals of *personnel coaching* deserve some brief comments. We'll discuss only the process to be followed when a poor or below-average rating has been attained.

Figure 10.   Employee performance review record.

Employee name _____	Clock number _____	Classification _____
Reason for appraisal _____	{Regular ____ {Special ____	Date _____

GENERAL CHARACTERISTICS	EXCELLENT	GOOD	AVERAGE	POOR
Attitude (enthusiasm, co-operation)				
Dependability (follows up, assumes responsibility)				
Knowledge of job (technical understanding; able to apply knowledge)				
Quality of work (accuracy, good appearance)				
Quantity of work (volume, speed, ability to stay up to date)				
Self-reliance (takes initiative, self-starter)				
JOB CHARACTERISTICS (Key dimensions of performance for each different job class in your office are entered here)				

The coaching environment. Frequently, your problem employees will enter a reviewing session with a negative attitude.

- They may be uncertain what behavior on the job is acceptable, and may feel that they are being singled out for criticism.
- They may feel resentment toward the person doing the appraising because they believe that discrimination is involved.

- They often anticipate that an argument could ensue, and if this happens, they normally will participate but typically expect to lose.

Any session that opens in such an environment can quickly go from bad to worse, unless these sentiments can be overcome. In the first place, the reviewer must start with a determination that the session will generate some positive results. The way to convert the employee to this frame of mind is to act in as supportive a manner as possible.

- Every action and mannerism of the reviewer should intentionally indicate empathy (rather than superiority).
- The site where the session takes place should be chosen for its "neutrality" (such as a conference room), rather than as a reminder of the boss's higher status (as would be the case in the reviewer's private office).
- When poor performance is to be discussed, only those performance details *which can be proved* should be stressed.
- If behavior problems appear to be involved, the reviewer should avoid passing judgment, either through direct statements or by implication.

The act of coaching. At the outset, it is important to remember that failed performance is less serious a fault than undesirable personal attitudes or work habits that would promote such failures. No one achieves satisfactory results 100 percent of the time. If results are consistently below par, the basic question is: *What is the employee doing wrong*, or *why is the employee's attitude wrong*? (Not, what went wrong?) Then, if it is possible to identify the defect, the employee must be told *how to do it right* or *how to act right*. That is the essence of coaching.

During the course of the session, the reviewer should be alert to various items of information that may be brought out and to any "contributory" comments—that is, situations the employee perceives as contributing to the problem.

- Are there office policies or work situations that interfere with good performance? If such is the case, the reviewer should make note of these and make a strong effort to get them corrected.
- Has the employee been informed directly about the desired outcome of his or her work? (You'd be amazed at how many office employees don't know this.)
- Does the employee need more on-the-job training to ensure good performance?
- A basic problem often comes to light—there may be no real disadvantage to poor performance. Someone else simply makes the correction. Referring back to the principle of the red-hot stove (discussed in Chapter 3), does the employee really get burned when he or she does something wrong?

Finally, the reviewer should have specifically in mind *what the management wants to happen* as the result of the session. This must be explained to the employee, and the reviewer should try (without coercion) to get him or her to agree that such an outcome is possible and desirable.

Employee Compensation

In many cases, office managers take the process of compensation for granted. It is an oversimplification to assume that the matter is settled when an employee has been informed that his or her salary will be such-and-such an amount of money. Instead, you should try constantly to "link" office requirements with the needs of individuals, so that each reinforces the other. If this can be done effectively, the employee's compensation package will be one of the best means of motivating top-notch performance. This will work only if you do a good

job of presenting the compensation factors to all employees on
the payroll.

How employees view compensation. Today's office worker
has a very complex attitude toward the money in his or her
paycheck. The following feelings are a common mix, compris-
ing employees' total feelings about compensation.

- Pay is a means of satisfying the employee's financial needs.
  However, many people's needs change with the passage
  of time. Thus, the leverage of this feeling can vary, depending on the employee's personal circumstances.
- Pay is an indication of individual importance to the organization. Of course, this reaction is most pronounced
  among the ranks of higher-paid employees. Also, it helps
  if employees know about differences in office salary grades
  and levels (not individual pay rates).
- Pay is a measure of progress toward an individual's private goals.
- Pay is a sign of equal treatment within the office. This is
  mostly a "negative" factor. Employees who are treated
  fairly usually take their salaries for granted, but employees who feel that others are getting a better deal will be
  very "demotivated" by their paychecks, no matter how
  sizable.
- Pay is a reward for work performed. *This is the reaction
  that will primarily be influenced by the compensation
  controls described in this chapter.* Although it is very
  basic, it is not necessarily stronger than the other reactions listed above.

How you can "upgrade" employee views. A large part of
this chapter has been devoted to a description of various out-
put-control approaches that will enable you to tie productivity
to office compensation. Here are some other factors to take
into consideration, as you attempt to get the performance you
are paying for:

- The expertise of office supervisors can greatly influence employee motivation and work attitudes. (This was discussed in the preceding chapter.) Have your supervisors actually *been trained to be a boss*?
- The office organizational climate can have a positive or negative effect. Do your policies and practices demonstrate a regard for people?
- Have the office jobs been organized to provide the greatest possible satisfaction or feeling of accomplishment? Work doesn't necessarily have to be disagreeable, as was indicated by the discussion of Theory Y in Chapter 3.
- Does job training in your office cease when employees learn the jobs they've been hired to do? Many people have an endless urge to learn more and to qualify for better jobs. Do you favor promotion from within, and if so, do your employees know this?

Conclusion

This chapter has described a number of ways in which the output of your office can be improved. Possibly some of these ideas are new to you; perhaps they sound theoretical or impractical. Some hard-boiled managers have even been known to say that "theoretical" is synonymous with "nonsense." On the other hand, it can't be denied that every practice, in all offices throughout this country, was new and untried at one time. So there is nothing wrong or "dangerous" about new concepts. The basic questions are: Can you profitably use a new approach? Would it be beneficial to your operation?

Here are some of the foundations for the recommendations contained in this chapter:

1. When the theories have been applied, they have generally produced good results.
2. These concepts have been useful in different situations.

In other words, they seem to be "universal," for the present state of the art.

3. The author has had sufficient past experience with the approaches to feel comfortable in predicting similar future results.

What can be more important to an office manager than the principal product of his or her office? Furthermore, to be sure of your influence over this product—the office output—there can be only one solution: you must find ways to control it. Generally speaking, control means an organized effort to ensure that you'll get the desired result by adopting various measures aimed toward that end.

The control of work in your office is quite similar to another form of control—personal self-control. To lose weight, to stop smoking, or to break some other bad habit involves hard work. It may take time, and for a while it may create new, unforeseen problems, but the end result is very worthwhile. You'll find the same thing when you try to control office output. You'll also find that such control is a key to effective operation of a profitable office.

5

Increasing
Office Profitability
Through Cost Control

Every office manager tries to keep costs low; many of them feel fairly comfortable with their present ratio of cost to office output. Would that describe your situation? If so, you might reflect for a moment on a "law" that was proposed a few years ago by a fellow named Parkinson. According to the good Professor Parkinson, *any given amount of work will expand to occupy the full time of those assigned to do it*. To evaluate what Parkinson said, can you recall a few situations in the past when you suspected that people were hoarding work, or where someone became expert at looking busy while actually doing very little? There might be more than a germ of truth in Parkinson's idea. However, this chapter could have been titled "Breaking Parkinson's Law." We will be examining a variety of ways to get a new grip on your office costs, and how to squeeze waste out of them. We'll be offering different perspectives. After some reflection, you should be better able to determine whether your people are spending their working hours in worthwhile effort.

Comparing Office Cost with Value

Every day, an office manager faces many problems. One of the most troublesome, which probably occurs fairly regularly for you, is trying to decide whether a particular activity is *really necessary* or if it would *just be nice.* That kind of a question could apply to a major function, now performed within the office, or it could relate to some new request or idea about work that is brought to your attention. In either case, the final outcome ought to be influenced by the "must factor"—*must* this be done? If there is more "maybe" than "must" when you analyze the necessity for the work, then the question is easily answered—don't do it. So, how do you balance the value versus the cost? Some perspectives on this issue are given below.

The Risk of Not Doing Something

Many offices perform costly paperwork to avoid a loss of a specific kind, but sometimes the *possible* loss could be less than the *certain* expense of doing the work. For example, would you allow a customer's claim without verifying it, on the assumption that most people are honest? Or would you agree that the customer should be reimbursed after only a cursory check, figuring that minimum verification is sufficient? If you answer "yes" to either of the above, you're violating a basic business principle. Keep necessary records. Use them to back up every decision. That's what administration is all about. Yet, in many offices, managers examine the value of all actions by figuring probabilities. They cost out alternatives. And frequently, they "bet" that it would be safe not to create records or establish procedures. Risky? Certainly. Any office system that is founded on the law of probability must accept a percentage of errors. Every assumption such as "most people are honest" will be wrong part of the time. In fact, some authorities call the practice of evaluating probabilities "risk management."

You can save money if you practice sensible management of risk in your office, but a word of caution is in order. When an office manager decides to take some risks, he or she ought to keep quiet about it. No point in worsening the odds by shouting what is being done to the world (or to employees who don't need to know). By being discreet about your risk management, you can help avoid abuse from opportunists and can concentrate on setting up some limits and controls regarding the acceptable level of risk. Here are some important points to keep in mind with regard to risk management:

• This approach doesn't mean abandonment of all records. Data should be kept and comparisons made. The *degree of detail* is the aspect that should be questioned.

• Simplification isn't necessarily synonymous with risk-taking. Any system of risk management will probably also involve simplification, but the reverse isn't necessarily true. For example, quite a few offices send blank checks to vendors when they issue a purchase order for a small number of items. This eliminates auditing the vendor's bill, and writing a check and mailing it. But the significant feature is *the risk of giving someone a blank check*, which says, in effect: "We trust you to fill in the amount we owe."

• Of course there should be limits to risk-taking. A few years ago, $100 was the common cut-off point. Now, with inflation, perhaps $250 would be better. Anything above that amount should be processed the "detailed way." But, many transactions in growing offices across this country don't amount to $50, let alone $100 or $250. What about yours?

To summarize, the risk-taking in your office (if you elect to go this route) should revolve around one basic question: *Is it less costly to suffer the consequences, or to maintain a system to avoid suffering those consequences.* When developing your answer to that question, consider the following: How much money is involved? How often does the circumstance occur? How much does the record-keeping cost? Or, to borrow a term from the professional gambler, "What are the odds?"

The "Exception Principle"

This administrative concept can best be explained by using a phrase that was common a few years back—"don't sweat the small stuff." A more dignified term, now in general business use, is "management by exception."

Basically, when you manage by exception, you do exactly that. There are no hidden meanings. You need only to designate the decisions to be made at your level, and what information you require before making such decisions. Then, you're ready. But that is the "small end of the horn." If *other managers who utilize most of the data generated in your office will* also *manage by exception, then you really have something.*

One thing which the author has learned from experience is that as the importance of business problems increases, the quantity of those problems should decrease. The clerk has more problems to solve than the office manager, but the office manager's problems have much more significance. And the same comparative statement applies to the problems of the office manager versus those of the chief executive of the company. Yet, the president of a certain company was once observed in the order department, sorting through the files and demanding to know the status of certain customers' orders. "What's holding this one up?" "Who authorized this special price?" "I want a report on this one by tomorrow morning." That wasn't an executive in action. That was an executive acting like a clerk.

What is suggested here is that an office manager sometimes must act like a missionary—trying to "save" the company from itself. He or she can greatly reduce the work done in the office, if other managers can be persuaded to *demand less information.* In any well-run organization, managers should concentrate on "unacceptable" situations, disregarding transactions that fall within the range of acceptability. The principle of focusing attention on those situations which exceed the acceptable range is illustrated in Figure 11. Of course, a primary target area will be the *reports* generated by your own office. Report-writing involves a good bit of work, so that's probably where you can find the best possibilities for elimination. Here's an illustration. The sales manager asks for a report of sales made by every salesman on the payroll. But all the salesmen have quotas, and as long as most of them are meeting their quota, why list that information for the sales manager? Why

Figure 11.   The flow of business transactions.

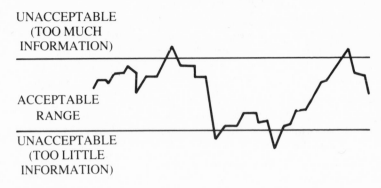

not propose that you give him a report of sales for only those salesmen below quota? Then, if business is good, your report can be very short and the sales manager's problems will be few. If business turns bad, you'll need to do more work to generate the report, and the sales manager will have many more headaches. That's management by exception.

If you try this approach, you'll probably encounter some opposition from your peers. Managers tend to be bothered by what they don't know. Some feel that they must constantly probe every detail, looking for errors or omissions. You must be able to assure someone like that that you have adequate controls, which will find all of the errors and omissions and bring them to the doubting manager's attention. In other words, you need proper record-keeping systems, and we'll get to that subject in Chapter 7. For now, the exception principle is proposed for your consideration as an ideal way to reduce both clerical work and office costs.

"Costing" of Office Activities

Back in Chapter 2, we spent some time exploring the importance of establishing a relationship between primary office objectives and numbers of office personnel. Now it's time to examine this subject from a dollars-and-cents standpoint. We can do this by analyzing costs and benefits.

The main steps of an office value analysis are as follows:

1. Establishing office goals, and determining how to staff the activities of the office (as discussed in Chapter 2)
2. Putting a dollar sign on each of those activities
3. Calculating the *benefit* of the work and comparing that to the *cost* you've computed

It all sounds rather cut and dried, but it isn't. During the evaluation process, an office manager must ask himself some searching questions. These are similar to the probing needed when you are making a risk-management or management-by-exception decision:

- Can we function if the work is eliminated?
- Does it cost more than it's worth?
- Is there a less costly method for doing the same thing?
- How much accuracy do we really need on this job?
- Could any of the work be done more effectively by some other part of the office (or even by an outside supplier)?
- Does this work duplicate some other office function?

The analysis, if properly done, is often based on a comparison—balancing the cost and quality of several alternative ways of accomplishing the end result. In other words, this is a *measuring process*: attempting to achieve what is necessary but at the least possible cost. Here's an example, taken from the author's consulting practice.

A particular client marketed a line of identifying rubber stamps. The client also assembled such stamps into kits, according to a customer's special needs. Inventories were kept on hand of complete kits of stamps, individual stamp holders, and many hundreds of small, molded rubber tips, which were to be glued to separate stamp holders by each customer. The cost value of the kits was in excess of $15. The stamp holders were valued at several dollars. However, the rubber tips were valued at a fraction of a cent apiece. Individual inventory records were maintained for every one of the above items. We proceeded to calculate the cost of this inventory record-keeping, and it became apparent that each separate stock of rubber tips was worth less than the clerical cost of day-to-day entries. In other words, the client was spending dollars to keep track of dimes. We stopped that waste by completely eliminating all inventory record-keeping for the rubber tips. Instead, a reserve supply of each tip was stored in its own brown paper "lunch sack," which in turn was held in the stock bin assigned to that particular rubber tip. Inevitably, the new method became known as the "brown bag" system. When all other rubber tips had been taken from the stock bin, the brown lunch bag was torn open; this permitted the reserve supply to be used to fill customer orders. Opening that brown bag was the stockkeeper's signal to start a shop order for production of more rubber tips.

This is an illustration of how inventory record-keeping—certainly a bona fide office activity—became wasteful because it was extended to the wrong type of item. The same kind of clerical misapplication can creep into your office, where it might be buried among the other costs of administration. Only your close scrutiny of every office activity can find and eliminate such useless expenditures. You will have to constantly compare costs versus values, in terms of office goals.

The Benefit of Office Administrative Standards

The dictionary defines a standard as a "carefully drawn specification." In practical terms, a standard is often used like a gauge—a way of measuring some activity or product that may or may not be within the range of acceptability. Administrative standards are presently an indispensable feature of all phases of manufacturing, but are *not* found in most growing offices. To be sure, *physical standards* are a common part of office life. For example, the paper used for letters and the envelopes that contain them have been standardized. Likewise, standards have been applied to many kinds of equipment used in offices; even the colors of the paint used to decorate office walls have been subjected to standardization. But the attitudes associated with the use of *administrative standards* are not congenial to a considerable number of office managers.

The final sections of this chapter, plus much of the remainder of the book, will deal with the reality that many things are easier to manage when they are uniform. However, before becoming specific, we will give some consideration to the general concept of standardization, as it pertains to the work of an office.

"Accepting" the Idea of Standardization in the Office

It is unfortunate that a good thing (the use of standards) first saw widespread acceptance as part of a bad thing (European war). Napoleon Bonaparte was the person responsible. That empire builder, that arch villain, that superb general, that great destroyer, was a real believer in the idea of "sameness." Wherever his armies conquered, he proceeded to standardize many phases of the society that had been defeated. That was one of the secrets of his military successes.

To switch to a more peaceful consideration of this subject, your office could derive the same prime benefit that Napoleon obtained from standardization. We are referring to the ability to specify *how you expect something to be done every time* in your office. This seems so beneficial that an observer might wonder why the heading at the beginning of this section refers to "accepting" the concept. Many managers do not utilize standardization, however. In the opinion of the author, the offices of most growing companies are not standardized to very great degree because *those businesses themselves were once considerably smaller.*

One of the final strongholds of managerial eccentricity can be found today embedded in the ranks of small business. That's not too surprising. If a rugged individualist can't tolerate working for someone else, he can always start a business of his own. Actually, this seems to be a healthy situation. Along with eccentricity comes innovation, and where would society be without the fresh ideas that generate so many new products and services? However, if one of those fresh ideas catches on with the public, and as the new product or service receives wider use, something else often happens. The small business, which supplies that new item, begins to grow. In direct proportion to the increase in business size and complexity, any rugged individualist who has a part in managing that company may become more and more out of place. With growth, it is much less practical for the business to cope with the inconsistent managerial styles and policies that an eccentric boss seems to favor.

From the author's experience, offices of many small but growing companies reflect a similar eccentricity and variability. Perhaps this is because managers of such offices learned their jobs in a simpler environment. Possibly there is some other explanation. In any case, a growing business office frequently remains *the last element of the company to accept the value of uniform operations.*

How do you feel about standardization? Consider your personal attitude: do you have doubts or reservations? If you are a true disciple, then you have already taken the first step toward installing as many uniform practices as possible in your office.

Introducing Standardization to the Entire Office

Once you have completely accepted the idea of managing as much as possible through the use of standard processes, you'll need to spread the good word around. You can't standardize alone. Many others in your office will have to understand and participate in this development. Unfortunately, quite a few people seem to resent an emphasis on preestablished or standard routines. As discussed earlier, if people are required to follow the same steps in an identical sequence time after time, they frequently feel insulted or diminished in some way. Back in Napoleon's day, he could overcome such resistance by threatening to have people shot if they deviated from standards; however, you will have to take a less direct approach. The best way is to try to sell the concept to the office work force.

The word "sell" is used advisedly. What you want is a favorable response to such terms as "increased effectiveness," "better service," and "greater job security." Whether you obtain such a favorable reaction will depend on how convincing you are in presenting the idea. *A growing office must eliminate as many exceptions as possible.* To fail to do this is to invite chaos as the office gets larger and larger. Reasonable workers can understand the value of greater efficiency. If they are taken into your full confidence, and asked to help establish job standards (as explained below), you may be astonished to see how acceptable the concept becomes to them.

The Control Process

To an office manager, the use of administrative standards can bring better control of costs—and greater profitability of operations. The way to achieve such a benefit boils down to three simple steps:

1. First, establishing the work standards
2. Then, measuring accomplishments or results, and comparing them to those standards
3. Finally, detecting and correcting any deviations

When you look at office management from the standpoint of cost control, you can readily understand the value of administrative standards. They are by far the best tool you can use in evaluating efficiency. Further, the results of such an evaluation can often be expressed in *both work units and dollars*. In the following sections, we'll talk about how job standards are derived, as well as the mechanics for applying them. To illuminate that discussion, it is necessary first to explore the connection between administrative standards, in general, and the control of office costs, in particular.

The Measurement of Job Performance

Every boss has certain expectations about the way work should be performed by employees under his or her supervision. Some bosses are very strict and critical. Others are much less so. But regardless of whether he is strict or lenient, a boss almost always develops some personal expectations or preferences about work. For want of a better term, we will call them "subjective work standards." About the only comment which applies to all such standards is that *they are not based on any uniform systems of measurement*. The author once knew a boss who said, "I want to hear those typewriter keys clicking, right up to 5:00 o'clock." For that particular individual, *the noise that a typewriter makes* was a satisfactory indication of acceptable performance. Another boss might say, "People should stay at their desks. I don't want to see them standing around the coffee maker, talking." Such a boss, then, could be said to feel that when employees are *sitting at their place of work*, they are keeping busy. You yourself may have a few pet subjective standards that have been imposed on the work of personnel in your office.

Of course, the trouble with any subjective work standard is that it doesn't necessarily have a predictable or constant relation to good work. The example of the boss who insisted on hearing the typewriter keystrokes is typical. Whether a typist was producing reports or correspondence, or simply typing "the quick brown fox jumped over the lazy dog" on scrap paper, the typewriter would make the same noise. Isn't there a better way to measure work performance than that? Certainly. The most accurate system is to set up job-performance standards and then to match the actual work with what each standard calls for.

The Nature of Work Measurement

A work-measurement program is simply a method of setting output standards in order to determine what a fair day's work should be. Although the approach doesn't produce 100 percent accuracy, it does eliminate the guesswork of enforcing subjective work standards. Further, you don't have to employ an industrial engineer to set office work standards. There are three simple tools for determining standards, which can be used by anyone:

> Records of past work performed
> Current time records or logs
> Work sampling

Here's what is generally involved. First, the work of a section of the office must be carefully surveyed and an orderly record must be made of the findings. For every *repetitive activity* of any significance, a time allowance must be established. Finally, a simple reporting system must be set up, so that each week or each month, every supervisor in that office section gets a report of verified production and time spent in carrying out the selected operation or operations. This will permit comparison of actual with standard.

Work Excluded from the Measurement Process

Obviously, not all types of office work can be measured. Nonroutine work—creative work, special studies, some types of technical duties, research, and so on—cannot be brought into the system. However, there are some jobs which, at first glance, seem to be of a nonroutine nature but which through careful study can be placed under a work-measurement program. For example, the author has been able to apply such standards to the work of engineering draftsman and collection correspondents. The secret, here, is volume—are there a considerable number of roughly similar steps to be taken? Sometimes, only a small part of an office job will be found to be unmeasurable, while that job had originally been considered too nonroutine to be included in work measurement. Even when work is truly nonrepetitive, a work-measurement study can still be valuable because it provides an analysis of the work steps required and a record of the amount of nonstandard output produced in the office.

Standards Based on Past Work Performed

Depending on the nature of the work and the reliability of key employees, it is often possible to reconstruct records of work completed in the past. Filed copies of reports or documents may provide everything that is needed. If such are not available, a supervisor plus a few "old-timers" can work together to make useful estimates. Though admittedly inexact, these estimates can be helpful by providing a base against which to compare future experience. They also isolate possible problem areas for further study. Were you aware that so much time was required for the work? Is the work worth it? The use of a simple estimate form, such as that shown in Figure 12, is recommended because it provides a written record for future reference.

Figure 12.   Work-time estimate form.

```
                    WORK-TIME ESTIMATE

    Position: _____ Date estimated: _____

                      Description  |  Estimated Weekly Hours

    Daily duties                   |


    Weekly duties                  |


    Monthly duties                 |


    Occasional activities          |


    Estimated by: _____ Approved by: _____
```

Take note that the employees whose work will possibly be standardized should be brought into the estimating process as often as possible. If they know what you are doing, and the reason why, their hostility and resistance will be minimized. And, as we have already stated, an office manager cannot standardize alone.

Standards Based on Time Records or Logs

If it proves to be impossible to establish the amount of work performed in the past, the current work information will serve just as well. Again, this approach will depend on the cooperation of the employees whose work is being analyzed. Every employee (not just a selected few) should be asked to maintain production records for a week—or longer, if the employee performs very many once-a-month jobs. Each record should be broken down according to the frequency of performance. A form such as that illustrated in Figure 13 is suggested as the medium for collecting this information. You will notice that information is required for the units of each kind of work turned out and the time needed to complete that work. Information regarding lunchtime, personal time, and unscheduled interruption times is also to be recorded. This record will provide a total time and task breakdown for each working day.

During the week or so while this information is being gathered, it is important to observe the work force from time to time to ensure that their work pace is about normal. The records should be turned in at the close of each day, and tabulated on the day after. In that way, it will be possible to detect discrepancies and to inquire about missing entries before the employee who is responsible has forgotten the details. A secondary benefit of this data-gathering will be the job profiles that will emerge. Also, it may be possible to detect excess time devoted to personal use, but unless the situation is flagrant, it is suggested that the offender not be confronted with his or her incriminating entries. If employees get the idea that the product of their cooperative effort is going to be used against them, you can forget about collecting any more relevant infor-

Figure 13.   Record of time spent at work.

```
┌─────────────────────────────────────────────────────────────┐
│                   EMPLOYEE RECORD OF                         │
│                   TIME SPENT AT WORK                         │
│                                                             │
│                                   Date _____            │
│   Name_____                        │
│                                                             │
│                                   Department _____         │
│   Position_____                       │
│                          │Units of│     │    │Total         │
│     Description of Duty   │ Work   │Begin│End │Time          │
│                          │        │     │    │              │
│                          │        │     │    │              │
│                          │        │     │    │              │
│                          │        │     │    │              │
│                          │        │     │    │              │
│                          │        │     │    │              │
│   Note: Include lunch period and       TOTAL ____           │
│   personal time in this record. Total                       │
│   of all times should equal your complete workday.          │
└─────────────────────────────────────────────────────────────┘
```

mation. On the other hand, you will be able to derive *an average* of the need for personal time, by taking the data from the time record for every employee. This personal time average can then be factored into the work-performance standards that you will be setting up at the end of the survey.

Standards Based on Work Sampling

This is the most disliked (and therefore the least satisfactory) of the three methods of compiling work-performance information. Employees do not relish having someone watch them at work, and that's what is required here. At random

Figure 14. **A random performance sampling form.**

RANDOM PERFORMANCE SAMPLING

Department _____ Date of Survey _____

Description of Work Surveyed	No. of Observations	% of Total	Time Required	Amount Produced

Surveyed by _____

times during the day, each employee is observed and the information is recorded on a form such as that shown in Figure 14.

This technique is based on the concept that a relatively small sample will produce about the same results as if the employees had reported all of their work. The method is mentioned here only because a number of authorities recommend it. The advantage claimed is a saving of time. The disadvantages, which the author considers to be serious, are twofold: (1) employees feel that they are being spied upon; (2) some people cannot perform naturally when they are being watched. ("If you're going to stand there looking over my shoulder, I'll never get this letter typed.")

Calculation of Standards of Output (Quotas)

Remember that a work standard is, in theory, what *an average employee* can accomplish in a given period of time.

Therefore, the raw data, gathered by any of the above procedures, are not usable directly. Instead, they must be compiled and the totals must be averaged, to reduce the degree of variations as much as possible. When you are satisfied that a particular number of work units is about what can be produced by one average worker in one hour, then by simply multiplying that figure times the number of work hours available, you arrive at the daily quota for that particular job. The same approach, followed for all other jobs that are to be included in the program, will complete the determination of work quotas. However, a word of caution is in order. In the author's experience, many mistakes can be made at this stage. Since these quotas are the basis of the entire work-measurement system, it is worthwhile to exercise great care and to recheck the reports and all calculations. Also, the standard amount of output can change with new equipment, new methods of work, or (sometimes) with new people.

The Work-Reporting System

In order to use the above information, you need a way to collect reports of work actually performed each day in the office. Here again, the cooperation of all employees is essential because they will have to produce the tallies of their output. At first there is generally some resentment and resistance, because some workers feel that preparing the work report is an added duty. Management must carefully and convincingly explain that from now on, the work report will be an integral part of the employees' regular jobs. It is very important to get this point across. Otherwise, preparation of the daily reports could become such an issue that the extra assignment of preparing all of them might have to be given to one employee.

A simple form such as that shown in Figure 15 can easily be designed for this purpose. Each worker should enter the data to the left of the vertical double line. The supervisor should make the entries to the right of the line.

Figure 15.   An employee performance report form.

EMPLOYEE PERFORMANCE REPORT
Name _____ Date _____
Position _____ Department _____

Work Description	How Counted	Quantity	Work Standard	Performance Efficiency

Calculated by_____

Uses of the Reported Data

It is possible for an enterprising office manager with an analytical mind to use the reports of work measurement to help solve many administrative problems, as well as to hold costs down. Sometimes, from the reports it appears that work should be reassigned, in whole or in part, in order to improve efficiency. By the time a work-measurement program has been successfully installed, some work is usually determined to be unnecessary. One of the author's clients had maintained the practice of same-day service in filling all customer orders. Since orders were received in fluctuating quantities on different days of the week, a fairly large staff had to be maintained, but some of the people were often idle. It was only after a work-measurement system had been installed that the office manager could show the dollars wasted by that same-day service policy. It was quickly changed by the top management, and one office manager felt very good about his accomplishment.

Using the Office Budget as an Administrative Standard

Today, budgets are important tools in growing offices. However, they are generally considered to be more of a financial record than an administrative standard. The reason for this fairly common opinion is that budgets are expressed in financial terms, and are based on data provided by the company's system of accounting. The author proposes the contrary argument that office budgetary reports are not solely meant to provide financial information. Instead, these records belong within the family of administrative controls that rely on standards to ensure that operations are carried out according to plan. In other words, according to this line of reasoning, a budget is *simply a financial standard*, a device for ensuring effective control over office costs.

Advantages of Budgeting

Let's consider all of the ways in which budgeting can help you do a better job of managing your office, and how it can serve to increase office profitability.

1. *More comprehensive administration.* One of the most significant advantages of budgeting is that the very process fosters an awareness of future problems and possibilities. You might not even take the time to think about such matters otherwise. It is understandable that you might avoid perplexing cost considerations in view of the many other demands on your time. All too often a sudden crisis will arise, forcing you to solve a cost problem by "shooting from the hip." In contrast, when you begin to develop formal budgetary plans for the future, and when the system makes it necessary to study deviations from these plans, you will become a much better manager. Your total approach to office administration will be more

consistent, and there will undoubtedly be fewer unexpected emergencies.

Another important benefit of budgeting is that every segment of your office will become involved. Each supervisor who is responsible for any phase of the office work will have to help you develop the budget. The result will be a consolidation of the thinking of key personnel, as well as your own thinking. Since budgeting will require the participation of supervisory employees, they are more likely to be "sold" on the concept and therefore more willing to abide by the end result.

Another general benefit of budgeting is that it gives you a way to formally express your office's financial policies. After you have completed a budget for the year and distributed copies to the employees responsible, they'll be better able to understand your intentions for that period. If you intend to cut back, your budget will indicate how much and where. If you plan to expand, the budget will clearly show your increased expense targets.

2. *Better controls.* As soon as your budgetary plan is prepared, you automatically possess a device for steering toward your goals. That is because what the office *does* can be easily measured against what it *was intended to do*. If your operation runs into trouble, you can take more precise corrective action. Your budget will be broken down into different elements, and one or more of those elements will contain the seed of the trouble.

In addition, when you spend money in accordance with a budget, it will be *controlled spending*. By carefully scrutinizing all projected costs before approving them, you can prevent waste. Of course, you will have to follow up any cost overruns; the budget can't police itself. However, with a budget, you can easily tell what part of the office was responsible for the excess costs.

3. *Improved coordination.* Having a better balance of different segments of your office will be another automatic by-product of budgeting. By drawing supervisors from all sections of the office into the preparation of the budget, you will pre-

vent any unit from expanding out of proportion or, equally important, from being ignored. The budget will ensure that each segment is allocated operating funds in proportion to its productivity or function.

4. *Summary of budgetary benefits.* Here are the general benefits you can expect your office administrative team to achieve from budgeting:

- A more organized and farsighted attitude toward the financial future of the organization, and the control of its costs
- Assurance that all responsible personnel have the same view of what the financial objectives are
- The ability to coordinate or consolidate diverse approaches toward the spending of money
- The possibility of analyzing how successful your financial planning for the future proved to be, and of determining what, if anything, went wrong

Human Reactions to Budgeting

In many offices, the "human problems" associated with budgeting require almost as much attention from the manager as do the analytical opportunities that the budgeting data provide. This is because budgets are often used to exert unfair pressures on the working staff, in the interests of efficiency. Make no mistake about it, office employees can learn to dislike the concept of budgeting just as rapidly and as thoroughly as they can begin to hate or fear a poorly designed work-measurement system. This reaction is the exact opposite of the cooperative spirit, and willingness to understand the company's position, which you ought to be trying to encourage. How people will actually react is almost entirely up to the management. Below are some important concerns regarding people's responses to budgeting.

There are three typical reactions that people exhibit when they encounter conflicts at work. The psychological terms for these reactions are aggression, regression, and fixation. An *aggressive* reaction to office budgetary controls is present when workers criticize the exercise of those controls excessively or when they directly retaliate with unnecessarily wasteful actions. The principal symptoms of a *regressive* response to the restrictions imposed by a budget are various forms of "doom and gloom" behavior in the office. A *fixation* against the unwelcome budgetary controls is present when workers become less and less congenial to financial restraints. They are fixated, so to speak, on the old, prebudgetary situation and are unable or unwilling to accept anything new or more restrictive.

This brief recitation of typical personnel reactions could be especially significant to you, if you have had to "crack down" recently by tightening financial controls in the office. Frequently, a legitimate exercise of fiscal restraint runs into extraordinary resistance because of past managerial misuse of the bugetary control process. Let's consider how some past actions on your part could be creating extra problems now. Then you'll know what to avoid in the future.

Recently, one of the author's clients saw an opportunity to comply with a budgeting directive from the head office without the change having a traumatic effect on the office personnel—or so he thought. At almost the same time that this manager's budget was cut, one of the older office workers developed a severe health problem and decided on an immediate early retirement. The salary which this employee was earning was almost exactly equal to the budgetary reduction that the office manager had been told to accept. "Great," he told himself, "we'll hold back a little on stationery and supplies cost and make up the rest of the cut by not replacing Charley." It seemed an ideal solution to the boss, but not to the other three people in Charley's section, who had depended on his effort to help make their output quotas. Almost immediately, two reactions occurred: the remaining workers referred to "that blankety-blank budget" and said "The boss thinks we've been goofing off." Perhaps the workers were at least partly correct in their second reaction; the office manager had occasionally said that the average level of productivity in his office was 70 percent, and had often expressed the opinion that "people could work harder if they wanted to." In any case, the section's adverse reaction to the lack of a replacement for Charley quickly spread across the entire office. The problem was compounded by the fact that Charley really had been making quite a contribution, and the section began to fall behind schedule within less than a week after he left. Here is what began to happen in the aftermath of the decision not to replace Charley:

- There was a decline in worker devotion to duty, as evidenced by a 3 percent increase in tardiness and absence.
- Daily output reports began to be "fudged" on almost a regular basis. The work-measurement system became replete with errors.
- It proved to be impossible to reduce the cost of stationery and supplies (as the office manager had intended). In fact, this cost went up slightly.
- There were several emotional outbursts during employee evaluation sessions, when the evaluator was trying to explore reasons for poor performance.
- The office manager began to feel that worker morale had been "shot to hell." He now says, "At the time, I couldn't understand what had happened."

What happened, in the author's opinion, was that the leverage of budgetary controls had been misapplied. It wasn't a fatal situation; the office as a whole was able to continue to function. However, the office manager certainly failed to consider the human factor when he decided not to replace Charley. In this particular case, there has been a happy ending. A replacement for Charley has been hired, but various administrative improvements have also been made that have lowered office costs. As a result, the office manager is still operating within his reduced budget.

From the above example, it is possible to reaffirm several principles:

- Budgetary controls are essential, as one of an office manager's administrative tools. However, if they are utilized in a way that can be interpreted as a whip instead of a carrot, human relations problems may occur.

- When workers are expected to increase individual productivity as the result of a reduction in staff, every effort should be made to persuade employees that their own best interest coincides with the need of the office (in this case, a need for financial constraints).
- The absence of good channels of communication, both down from the office manager to the workers and up from the workers to the manager, will create severe managerial problems in times of trouble.

Conclusion

The contribution that an office can make toward profitability will usually be concentrated in two areas—better use of resources, and improved productivity. This chapter has dealt with both. One of the prime resources of any growing office is people, starting with you as manager and proceeding down to a messenger boy. Another very important resource, of course, is money, and no office ever has enough of that. What we have tried to do in this chapter has been to consider various ways that people (including you) can be utilized more effectively and also ways in which money can be saved. No two growing offices are alike—thus, there is a wide variety of cost-control approaches that can be taken. However, the so-called bottom line ought to be the same in every case: greater efficiency of office operations.

A successful office can be considered (among other things) to be a complex social system. You need more than competent people to achieve efficiency. You need interdependent relationships within the working force, with each person supporting the other. That is why a quest for cost saving on your part will be either handicapped or reinforced, in proportion to the number of other people in the office who join you in that quest. If you have wondered why so much attention has been devoted to office employees' feelings about job standards, budgets, and so forth, this has been because their interaction with these programs is so vitally important.

The passage of time is another key factor. If you fail to get the expected results from what seems to be a very good cost-saving possibility, the reason could be that insufficient time has been allowed. Frankly, a longer time interval is often needed than is generally anticipated. Office improvements tend to start out slowly, then are likely to continue to grow steadily in significance until a favorable level of improvement is reached.

In summary, then, you can definitely enhance your ability to exercise office cost control. You might need to master changed principles of management. You might have to become more responsive to interpersonal relationships. But either or both of these behavior modifications should be possible for you. What you must have is the urge to improve, and the willingness to continue your effort over a long enough time period.

6
The Significance
of Quality Assurance
for Office Management

Generally, when the term "quality" is used with respect to business, it brings to mind such comments as "they don't make 'em like they used to" or "if Japan can produce a great small car, why can't we?" In other words, good or bad quality is usually associated *with a product*. However, you surely would acknowledge that poor workmanship could occur in an office, just as frequently as in a factory. In fact, since white-collar personnel have outnumbered blue-collar workers in the United States for the past twenty years, it stands to reason that there are *more instances of clerical blunders than of production errors*. So, what can be done about it? People make mistakes; "to err is human."

Well, since the workmanship of those people who are employed on a production line can be improved (and this is presently occurring all over the country), then why can't office personnel achieve a higher rate of accuracy? The answer is—of course they can. This chapter will discuss ways of bringing about this happy outcome. Occasional references will be made to production situations, and offices and factories will sometimes be compared. The reason for such references is that the quest for better quality first came to prominence with respect to *things*, not services. There are a whole host of activities in production facilities that have a quality orientation—such functions as dimension inspection, metal fatigue testing, material control, quality assurance checkpoints, and the like. But with respect to office work, there are fewer equivalent activities. In other words, office workers today usually find and correct their own mistakes, because there's no one else assigned to do it.

Who Should Be Responsible for Quality Workmanship?

It is not being suggested that an office manager should hire personnel whose sole duty is inspection of clerical output. No, by and large, office employees should undoubtedly continue, as in the past, to be their own inspectors. And since these workers report to the office manager either directly or through one or more intermediate layers of supervision, then *the responsibility for the quality of office work falls directly on the person at the top*. There's no other way to look at it.

In a production situation, part of the duty to improve quality must be given to the function that designs the product. An article must have quality "built in"; quality can't be added to a basically poor product by a series of tests or inspections. Translating this responsibility into a clerical situation could raise an interesting question—who "designs" the work in your office? Is it you or some other boss? Or has the chore been assigned to a specialist of some kind? And who is privileged to make changes or improvements? This subject will be discussed later in the chapter in regard to quality circles. For now, it's sufficient to bring up the question of who should be in charge of quality. In many offices, quality assurance is such an "orphan" that no one is charged with the overall responsibility for ensuring that every phase of the work is of the appropriate quality—well designed and well executed.

Why Do Office Employees Make Mistakes?

Let's begin by dispelling a belief that is very popular with bosses. Except in rare cases, an employee does not prove to be error-prone solely because of an "I couldn't care less" attitude. Office employees, as a group, tend to be as conscientious as you would want them to be. The fault—the reason for most employee mistakes—can be traced to inadequate fulfillment of responsibility by some member of management. Consider the following reasons for the majority of office mistakes:

> Poor working conditions
> Lack of proper training
> Ineffective communication
> Insufficient advance planning
> Improper work specifications
> Poorly designed procedures or forms
> Erroneous scheduling
> Inattention to detail

Only the last reason on the list (serious though it is) can be traced to an employee attitude. With all of the others, the clerical worker is powerless to correct the situation, and must try to cope with a less-than-perfect working environment.

Administrative Control of Office Errors

Not all clerical errors can be prevented, unless you are willing to spend a great deal of money in the process. However, it is certainly possible for an office manager to reduce the percentage of erroneous office work. There are several possible ways to go about it.

A Formal Error-Control Program

A realistic goal for a formal program would be to *lower the number* of errors that employees make, by some substantial percentage. And the time for such a program to begin would be when each new employee starts his or her first day in the office.

Emphasize quality. When an employee is trained, he or she should learn both how to do the job, and what constitutes acceptable work. After an employee has become adept at performing a clerical operation, it quickly becomes a matter of habit. Before long, the task that first was a challenge, and therefore interesting, gets to be familiar and is regarded simply as more of the same old thing. As a result, many employees don't consider their work important. That's when emphasis on quality becomes essential, because at this point the percentage of errors will otherwise begin to grow.

Establish acceptable limits. You need to decide how far from perfection the work can be, while still regarded as acceptable. This simply is the point at which the probable cost of a mistake exceeds the expenses of catching it. Obviously, different kinds of office work would justify a greater or lesser degree of care in performance, and more or less accuracy in the end result.

Help each worker to take a user's viewpoint. People who do the same thing every day tend to lose respect for their work. In fact, they often take for granted the fact that mistakes will occur, and therefore they feel no regret at making errors. Employees often get a real shock from learning the trouble and cost that some of their mistakes can create. This is best illustrated by written complaints (often solicited by the boss) that explain what the user intends to do with the work, and how much of a handicap poor work can be.

Set up a correction procedure. When an unacceptable level of errors is first detected, a corrective series of actions is called for. (Such a series is established *in advance*.)

1. Recheck the worker's training, to be sure that he or she understands how much quality is required on the job.
2. Show the worker some examples of unsatisfactory work. Explain exactly what is wrong, and the significance of the mistake.

3. Make a permanent record of each error that is serious enough to require the above steps.
4. If you consider it justifiable, start the practice of having some member of supervision make periodic quality checks.
5. Include a provision for quality performance to be recognized when raises in pay or promotions are being considered.

Statistical Quality Control

This involves a different approach, which has seldom been applied to office work but which is absolutely vital to large-scale production of material goods. There is a basic reason for the popularity of statistical quality control. *It pinpoints quality problems quickly and forms the basis for taking corrective action.* Also, *the cost is much less* than would be the case for a rigorous total inspection program, but the *results are virtually the same.* With statistical quality control, a quantitative-analysis approach (in other words, the application of statistical methods) is used for controlling the quality of work. There is still the need for subjective judgments—both by the boss and by the worker—but statistical controls can help both parties turn out higher-quality work.

Some people wonder whether this technique can be applicable to office work. It can indeed: statistical quality control is just as applicable to many kinds of office work as it is to factory work. As a matter of fact, the most widespread use of statistical sampling (the foundation of all statistical quality control) takes place in the U.S. Bureau of the Census, where there is no assembly line or output of material goods and where the only commodity in use is sheets of paper. However, before this form of quality control can be put to use in an office, the management will have to absorb some of the principles of statistical analysis.

Statistical methods, as explained below, can be applied to the control of clerical work only after someone decides *what quality of work is acceptable.* The term "acceptable" does not mean complete freedom from mistakes; it merely signifies a predictable and controllable level of accuracy. Once that degree of quality is established, the use of statistical methods can ensure that the selected percentage of error-free work is uniformly and dependably maintained.

When a level of quality is being decided on, the basic decisions relate to costs and benefits. What cost would be associated with producing work that is 90 percent free from error, for example? How much more would it cost to raise the level of error-free work to 95 percent? What would be the increase in benefits that the more accurate work would provide? These are administrative questions that can't be answered in the abstract, *but they must be carefully considered for each distinct kind of clerical work.* Then, no matter what degree of accuracy is selected, the quality-control system should be monitored carefully and regularly to see that it is holding to the selected level. That's statistical quality control.

One way to carry out such monitoring is through the practice of statistical sampling. Periodically, certain work is "sampled"—selected from a larger lot of the same work. The *size* of the sample and the *frequency* of selection are considered crucial to the success of this approach. In fact, unless the statistical sampling is carefully done, it can easily lead to false conclusions. Following are some important points with regard to sampling.

Sample size. The purpose of taking a sample of the work is to establish the accuracy of the whole batch. With the *random* approach, the larger the sample, the more realistically it will represent the character of the complete lot. Realism has been found to increase in proportion to the square root of the sample size. Thus you would get, for example, a 10 percent improvement in reliability by increasing the size of the sample by 100.

Frequency. A different sampling approach could be called the *systematic* method. With this method, you take individual samples at regular intervals. You could, for example, make a detailed check of every 10th invoice, in order to determine the acceptability of the whole day's output. This, in other words, involves the *frequency* of sampling. To get started with this method, you refer to a "Table of Random Numbers" (found in most college algebra textbooks) to decide the identity of the first invoice. Suppose the "Table of Random Numbers" has 5 as the first integer. You then select the 5th invoice, the 15th, the 25th, and so on, if you have decided on a frequency of 10.

Uniformity. The most important aspect of sampling has to do with the use of a *standard plan.* You must decide the best way to take samples of a particular kind of work, and then stick to that method. If you change from one approach to another from time to time, you destroy the reliability of the statistical sampling process—thus, you reduce the possibility of there being long-range control over work quality through the use of sampling.

Sometimes, samples taken from a batch of office work—say, typed follow-up letters or copies made on a duplicating machine—may be *better than acceptable.* In such a case, you could actually find a *deviation on the plus side* when you take a sample. Statisticians call these situations two-sided probabilities. The significance of a two-sided probability, as opposed to a single-sided type, is that the good could entirely or partly cancel the bad. Thus, in a two-sided example, you might have an unacceptable level of error that is partly offset by some better-than-necessary work. If you go into statistical sampling, be most careful to determine whether departures from the level of acceptability can be one- or two-sided. If you're dealing with the latter, be sure to take separate counts and *use only the bad work* when calculating the degree of acceptability.

Error Prevention Through Employee Participation

In attempting to reduce mistakes in office work, an entirely different approach is to solicit advice from the workers. Let the people who turn out the work tell you how it could be made better, or easier to do and therefore more error-free.

A well-known process called the "suggestion system" was developed years ago for exactly that purpose. Many offices have installed such a system and have obtained good results.

It's been a different story in other offices, however, where the suggestions turned in have either been few or mostly impractical. The difference seems to be in the attitude of the worker and in the office manager's reaction to suggested improvements. For a wide variety of reasons, some offices could be described as a "happy ship," but others could not. Whatever the case, a suggestion system relies on *voluntary* participation.

In the past few years, a somewhat similar concept has attracted considerable attention across the country. It is known as "quality circles" because a group solution developed by a number of workers (a "circle" of people) is applied to important problems encountered on the job. The similarity between a suggestion system and a quality circle rests on the fact that an idea from the work force is used to solve a management problem. The difference between the two methods relates to the degree of advance preparation that management applies to either process—very little with a suggestion system but quite a lot for quality circles. The remainder of this chapter will be devoted to the possible effects of quality circles on office work.

Quality Circles Applied to Office Work

The solution cycle contained in Figure 16 depicts the typical functioning of a quality circle. Note that during the problem-solving process, there is considerable interaction between the office management and the workers. It is this level of interaction and cooperation which can make or break the process, particularly because the solution of one problem often creates another one (as Figure 16 illustrates).

These problem-solving steps will be discussed further. First, however, it is appropriate to consider "management readiness." That is, decision-makers at the head of the organization must be prepared to support ideas proposed by each quality circle. In other words, management should be ready to accept the proposition on which this whole concept is based—namely, that workers can produce worthwhile improvements for the benefit of the company. Management readiness must:

Figure 16. A problem-solving cycle.

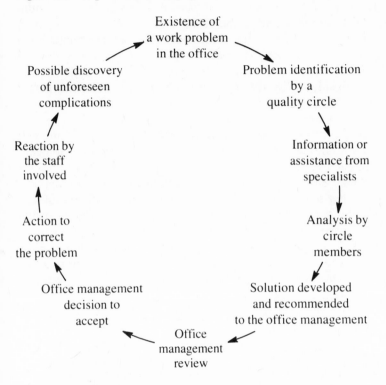

- Come *from above*—that is, from the head of the organization or someone close to him.
- Be "in place" *before* the quality circle concept is introduced.
- Be well *understood* and *accepted* by the work force. If the workers lack confidence in the readiness of management, they will see no point in participating in a quality circle.

The Anatomy of a Quality Circle

In offices where this approach is used, a quality circle typically is composed of three parts.

- A *facilitator* is responsible for the overall functioning and success of the concept. This person is generally in a middle-management position and acts as a go-between, linking members of the circle with various members of management. When some type of improvement or solution to a problem has been developed by a quality circle, the facilitator arranges to have it considered by the appropriate manager, and takes part in installing acceptable improvements.

- A *leader* is charged with leading members of each circle, keeping them oriented toward improving a troublesome situation, and acting as a spokesperson for the group. The leader of each circle is a key person; he or she can greatly help or totally ruin the entire approach. A leader must be adept at solving office problems and must know how to communicate and motivate. A leader must also be a team builder (as will be discussed shortly) with an understanding of group dynamics. Leaders are generally drawn from the rank and file of workers and then given special training. A good quality circle leader often becomes promotable, as the result of experience gained in leading his or her circle.

- A *member* is simply a worker who has volunteered to participate in a quality circle. Members must be given the same kinds of training as leaders, but not to the same degree of intensity. A good member should display two principal characteristics: (1) interest in the proper functioning of the office, and (2) a good general understanding of how the office operates (what work is done when and by whom). In short, an effective quality circle member can be any good *and* experienced worker.

To be successful, a quality circle should meet regularly; at least once a week is the generally accepted schedule. Each meeting should be expected to last one to two hours. Unless meetings are held on company time, the whole approach will quickly break down. Obviously, quality circles require mental work. If a worker is expected to work hard after hours, for the good of the office and without extra compensation—well, there are probably a few people in some offices who would do it, but seldom enough to constitute a quality circle. A good test of "management readiness" is the willingness of the office manager to pay the workers to function as a quality circle.

The meetings held by a quality circle are best governed by a set of rules, adopted by the workers themselves and modified from time to time as warranted by circumstances. Members should function as a group, do things together that couldn't be done alone, and draw upon one another's special knowledge or abilities. In other words, a quality circle can't simply be a mob or a bunch. It is supposed to do more than provide members with an opportunity for a gripe session or the chance to gossip. A quality circle, above all, must be a *team*, committed to making improvements in the activities of the office.

The Need for Team-Building

Most people are competitive by nature: practically everyone likes to win. This drive to win may be *at the expense of* or *with the help of* other people. When workers are formed into a team, they are potentially in a position to help one another to win. Some teams become destructive, however. Members who are competitive with each other prior to the team's establishment may continue their attitude, in which case the team may work at cross-purposes. Further, workers on one team may try to tear other teams down. The objective is for all teams to work in concert to benefit the whole organization. This phenomenon won't happen accidentally. What we're driving at is the development of a win-win attitude on the part of team members and between quality circle teams in an office.

The Development of Quality Circle Teams

A quality circle should represent a distinctive way for employees to solve problems by working together. The aim should be to harness the collective energy and the various talents of the circle members. A *team* can be considered a flexible tool that emphasizes exploration and self-development of the members, while at the same time striving for the good of the organization.

Not all groupings of employees are teams, however. People can form a working group without taking on the characteristics of a team. Members of such a group, for example, might simply be trying to protect themselves from blame. They could even be attempting to prevent something from occurring rather than working to make it happen. Following are some characteristics of true teams:

Results. Unless a team can produce some results, why bother with it? In fact, the best test of whether a team formation really has taken place is found in the answer to a hypothetical question, "What has this group really accomplished?" If there are desirable results, you can bet that some type of team has been formed.

Goals. A team must have a purpose that is understood and sought after by the whole group. This is another key characteristic of teams.

Synergy. Team members, by working together, can be said to have developed "synergy." The word means that extra dimension of energy which becomes evident when people are trying to achieve something together.

Structure. As a group, a team must be able to produce answers to such questions as "Who's in charge?" and "How do we go about accomplishing our goals?" A team organization should be orderly, and team members should respond to pressures in a uniform way. However, the team structure should be flexible rather than rigid.

Spirit. Team spirit reflects the quality of the team's work. If the work is good, the members feel proud of it. They are then said to have good team spirit.

Identity. Team members should "know that they belong" to the team. They generally are willing to try a little harder in the name of the team, and certainly they can feel proud to be part of it.

Collective learning. Teams must learn together, and their collective knowledge will then "belong to the team" even though each member has retained the experience individually. To help in the learning process, team members often ask one another such questions as "What results have we achieved?" and "What goals have we set up? Have we reached them?" Teams must answer difficult questions and be able to solve hard problems, while always working together. When a group that originally was just a list of names on a sheet of paper actually takes on a personality, team-building has really occurred.

Stages in Team-Building

In the author's experience, the progress made by teams has seldom been orderly or predictable. However, there is a process which can almost be called a pattern of growth. By the time the process is complete, a team has emerged.

1. *Getting acquainted.* People who are brought together in a group usually try to "find their place" in it. Some are outgoing and seem to be trying to dominate; others are reticent and appear to be timid. There is a very large and as yet unanswered question in the mind of each person: "How do I fit in?"

2. *Maneuvering for control.* Before long, there is a period of "testing." Relationships begin to be formed, and a few group members stand out as especially influential. For most teams, someone will have been formally appointed to act as leader. During this stage, the formal leader must be seen as dominant by the rest of the group; otherwise, the quality of teamwork will be poor. It is interesting to observe a group during the maneuvering stage. Most members are trying to find a way to work together, yet they still have an unanswered question: "Who's in control?"

3. *Resolving the control issue.* As soon as a leader of the team is accepted, the team can get to work. That's when quality circle progress will begin to take place.

Management's Contribution to Team-Building

From the foregoing discussion, you may get the impression that teamwork and team spirit must develop spontaneously within the group. That is exactly the case. Teams build themselves as the group learns to work together and as soon as the question of leadership is resolved. However, there are several things that an office manager can do in order to encourage the formation and growth of teams.

Promote the idea. Since quality circle members are typically drawn from various parts of the office, who is to say that they should become a team? If the office manager won't say it, you can be fairly sure that a team will seldom be formed.

Be patient. The building of a team takes time. You could compare the development of an effective team with the operation of an efficient engine. When a new engine is started up for the first time, it's far from efficient. There has to be some tinkering with it. The parts must begin to wear against each other and rough spots have to be smoothed. It's the same with a team.

Be supportive. As previously explained, team spirit develops when team members perceive themselves as productive. For a quality circle team, this occurs when the group has come up with an improvement and when *management has accepted it*.

How Quality Circle Projects Can be Selected

In every office, there are many conditions that can be improved by quality circle study. Normally, the most fertile area for correction is work defects. To identify problem situations, watch for the following clues:

- Work must frequently be done over.
- Due dates are often missed.
- Employees repeat the same error many times.
- Customers complain frequently about the same thing.
- Other parts of the office are adversely affected in a uniform way.
- Work is repeatedly incomplete.
- Procedures are generally ignored.
- Cost overruns are common. (This is the most important phenomenon to watch for.)

Another way to locate defective work is to call the attention of a quality circle to any of the problems described in the list on page 133.

How Quality Circle Improvements Affect the Office

If you decide to invest time, effort, and money in a quality circle program, *and if you do so properly*, you can expect both tangible and intangible benefits.

Tangible benefits. If you try to measure actual cost reductions, you'll be asking for trouble. Most office work is an ongoing process, with few discrete steps that lend themselves to being costed. That's why it is so difficult to determine the cost of such activities as processing an invoice or posting an entry. But consider another approach to the same end. Why not try to *measure results*? The following items can easily be measured:

- Improved customer service and fewer complaints
- Elimination of work bottlenecks
- Significant time savings
- Fewer errors to be corrected
- More effective procedures (i.e., procedures that can be and are being followed)

Intangible benefits. A good quality circle program brings about an improvement in employee attitude that cannot be measured but is very noticeable to any perceptive office manager. Also, such things as reduced absenteeism or fewer grievances (which are easily measured results) will flow directly from improved worker attitudes. When office personnel begin to be aware that work improvements generated by other employees have been accepted and are being implemented by the management, the effect on morale can be almost magical.

Conclusion

The theme of this discussion has been that the quality of office work *depends on the worker*. No office manager and no re-checking system can possibly put quality into the work. The only individual who can do that is the person who *does* the work. Thus, every system of quality control is founded on two basic requirements—each office worker must be taught to *care about quality*, and that worker must also be trained and assisted in every possible way to *produce quality output*.

Also, as we have said, "quality" does not mean perfection. It means the proper level of freedom from mistakes required by a particular kind of work and a specific use of the product of that work. The final decision as to quality should be the result of a compromise between what an office manager wants and what he or she is willing to pay to get it. Any other policy regarding office work quality is not practical or economical.

Finally, let's stop for a moment and consider the term "quality control." The general meaning of "control" is associated with a managerial activity, but the *control of quality* requires delegation. Management doesn't perform the actual work; thus, management should be freed from as much detail as possible from the standpoint of quality. However, an office manager must retain a means for assuring that the final result—acceptable work—is within prescribed limits. The way to achieve this is through preestablished methods, procedures, and policies. With such an approach, control does not necessarily reduce the creativity of work efforts. Instead, it serves to direct and guide the worker. Which brings us, full circle, back again to the individual on the job as the key ingredient in quality control.

7
Improving Office Profitability by Controlling Forms and Systems

The most common activity in a growing office is the recording of information. Take a good look at your office. Notice how many employees are using keypunch equipment, accounting machines, typewriters, adding machines, and so on. You may even find a few people who are using pencil and paper. But, no matter what kind of equipment is being utilized, the *users are recording data.* You might say that such a thing is to be expected, because, after all, an office is where most clerical work is done, and clerical work usually requires writing some kind of information. If you make a statement like that, you're right. Or to be more exact, you're half right.

Not all clerical writing serves a useful purpose. When clerical writing is performed effectively, *original data are recorded.* That's good. When clerical writing is performed inefficiently, *data are copied.* That is probably bad—bad because this process can be wasteful and quite possibly unnecessary. Systems analysts use the word "transcribing" when they describe the operation of copying information from one form to another. However, transcribing involves more work than this. When an office employee copies, other clerical actions are also required. The employee must search for the needed data at the source, read it, and verify that it has all the characteristics of the information to be entered a second time. He or she must then select the correct location for the copied entry, write it down, and check the written entry by proofreading. Both mental and physical efforts are involved, and of course there is always the chance that some kind of error will be made.

To avoid clerical transcribing and many other unnecessary activities, several conditions are necessary. These conditions may or may not be present in your office. They are *organized forms control* and *systems study*. This does not mean taking an informal or haphazard approach to checking on forms or procedures that appear to be extremely inefficient. Nor does it refer to the application of control measures just once, when each new record-keeping system is installed. Either of these administrative steps would be inadequate—the same as plugging only the worst leaks in a boat and then throwing away your bailing bucket. No, the only way to reduce procedural waste and the number of forms used in your office is to set up a regular system and to assign functional responsibility and authority over *all forms* and *all procedures*. That's how to cut costs and increase office profitability. This chapter will be devoted to that subject.

The Concept of a Record-Keeping Systems Cycle

If just one writing operation and then another is studied, only a few wasteful practices at a time will come to light. The way to overcome inefficiencies in wholesale lots is to *consider a complete record-keeping system cycle*. The concept of such a cycle is considerably simpler than it sounds. Clerical work originates at one point in the office and generally is completed at another point, with some valuable result being accomplished. Several people are involved; a few forms are filled out.

Here's an example. One of your company salesmen could begin a system cycle by taking a customer's order and writing it up on an order form. He sends the order to the office, where various employees process it. Eventually, the items are shipped to the customer and someone sends out a bill. When the customer makes payment, this particular cycle is complete. You could call it "the sales cycle." The transaction could involve a number of clerical steps: (1) order, (2) withdraw from stock, (3) ship, (4) invoice, and (5) collect.

Now, stop and reflect about this transaction. What items of information did the salesman write? Different people within the office worked on this order, using information that the salesman supplied and adding more data of their own. Where did these people work? The sales office; the credit department; the order acceptance desk; the shop; the stockroom; the shipping office; the shipping dock; the billing department; the cashier. How many items of information "flowed" the entire length of this system? How many were added along the way? Thirty? Fifty? Even one hundred? How many were copied onto one form and then another? How often did this happen? If multicopy forms had been used, could some of those transcriptions have been eliminated? Did all of the work stations need to know all of the information? Why? Might there be some completely different process that would accomplish the same result at a reduced cost? What we've described here is the kind of thought process that is called "system analysis."

Furthermore, changes in the system cycle in this example (which deals with processing a customer's order) could *also* affect the record-keeping required for finished goods ordering, producing and storing (another systems cycle), cash receiving, recording, and management (still another). In fact, as illustrated in Figure 17 one of the characteristics of effective system study is that *very widespread changes* in record-keeping will often result from *very small beginnings*. In the figure note that changes in Cycle 1, for instance, can affect Cycles 2 and 3.

While the study and improvement of record-keeping sys-

Figure 17.   Many systems cycles are tied together.

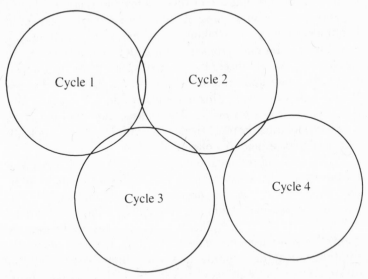

tems is very important to every company, this is *not* the kind of activity for a manager of a growing office to personally undertake. It might look easy; it might be tempting to make a few changes that correct obvious problems. But the value of such improvements will be minor in comparison to what probably should be done. (In the author's experience, growing offices are unusually susceptible to clerical inefficiencies.) The magnitude of the effort required to introduce large-scale changes will necessitate a full-time assignment, and that's too much for any office manager to handle. So you'll have to make a choice—let someone else have full responsibility for improving the systems of your office, or accept the reduced level of improvement that your part-time effort can produce.

The Proper "Systems Role" for an Office Manager

Today, the conduct of business in our society has progressed to a stage often called "the age of management." The term simply means that hired managers, instead of actual owners, now conduct most business affairs. This situation usually begins to develop as soon as a company starts to grow. Both opportunities and problems become increasingly plentiful, while the talents of the founders of the business are stretched thinner and thinner.

A common myth is that "a manager can do anything." No matter what the problem, a manager can solve it. Whether there's a need to build a better camera than the Japanese or Germans, or to overcome technological difficulties that took twenty years to develop, or to operate at a profit in the middle of the recession—some manager somewhere could make those things happen if he or she really wanted to. No job is too difficult; there is no obstacle that couldn't be overcome. The general public and nonmanagerial workers may regard the office manager in this light, since the latter is a member of an organization's management group. In keeping with such an impression, it may be felt that an office manager should become deeply involved in eliminating clerical inefficiencies by studying the record-keeping systems carried out in his or her office.

The author has already taken the position that this activity is not a proper one for an office manager. Not only is systems study quite time-consuming, *it is also a staff function* that requires special knowledge and skill. Refer back to page 23 for some comments about staff authority. At that point, it was recommended that staff actions should *assist or supplement* line activities. So an office manager, acting appropriately out of the line role, works with, seeks help from, and facilitates staff systems study in every possible way. That's quite different from actually trying to accomplish such studies; it's also the way to achieve the best results in terms of profitable performance of office functions.

A nontechnical description of office managerial duties would encompass the following:

1. *Overseeing work performance.* Making certain that desired operations are performed in the prescribed way; ensuring employment of proper equipment and forms;

checking to see that jobs are completed within the allotted time.

2. *Making plans and decisions.* Determining what future actions are needed and what personnel should perform them; deciding what current problems are to be solved and in what ways.

3. *Evaluating the performance of office work.* Considering what has been performed and how effectively it has been done; determining whether work should be done in an even better way in the future.

Only a few of the above duties have a system implication, as opposed to the much greater range that are purely administrative in nature. Thus, it's easy to understand where an office manager's primary focus of attention should be. Although the importance of improving record-keeping efficiency can't be ignored, an office manager can make the greatest contribution *by appraising the result of someone else's effort.*

Selection of "Targets" for Systems Study

A major feature of an office manager's facilitating role is in selecting the trouble spots where staff system study will do the most good.

1. *Time considerations.* In diagnosing record-keeping ills, one significant symptom is the *amount of time* required for completion of specific clerical work. Excessive lengths of time usually point to a "sick" procedure or system.

2. *Growing-volume considerations.* This factor may be considered as one of the best indications of current inefficiency. Although a procedure may have originally been well conceived and established, it will quickly become obsolete if the *volume of work* increases appreciably. In such cases, there is often a need either for more mechanization or for policy changes that will result in elimination of some phases of the record-keeping.

3. *Expense considerations.* Although this consideration is

simply a reflection of either of the above problems, it is often the easiest to recognize. The troublesome details of some office jobs may be obscure; however, they can be spotted quickly through an examination of costs. For example, a growth in salary expense or in the cost of supplies purchased may signify all sorts of procedural difficulties.

Types of Systems Assistance

A number of different approaches to office systems improvement are in vogue today. Each type offers the office manager a different kind of assistance; therefore, it is common (and certainly to be recommended) that several different methods of attack be used concurrently within a growing office. So long as the possible benefit of each type is well understood, there need be no fear of overlapping. On the other hand, a *misapplied* type of system improvement may be worse than none at all. In such a case, the commotion caused by the study can easily be confused with desired results. After the money is spent and the dust has settled, the office manager may discover that no real improvement has been made.

Work Simplification

This technique has been generally defined as a commonsense program designed to inject efficiency into and eliminate wastefulness from regular clerical operations. The practice of work simplification in the office is not at all new. You can be certain that as soon as clerical records began to be maintained, perhaps as far back as the beginning of recorded history, human ingenuity was devoted to working out shortcuts or improvements. We may feel a degree of envy for an "office manager" of those ancient days. Without automation, air conditioning, or coffee breaks, office life must have been relatively simple. Remarkably, there was virtually no difference in the approach to office work simplification from the earliest times until the beginning of the twentieth century. With the pioneering of Frederick W. Taylor, however, as well as with the work of Henry L. Gantt, the Gilbreths, and other proponents of scientific management, the unorganized or "tinkering" approach to work simplification—unorganized in the sense that there is no *overall plan* for systems improvement—has taken on almost a codified status.

The approach to office work simplification may be very simple and informal, or it may be more elaborate and formal, depending on the office manager's wishes and the resources available to him. In the "informal" plan, all employees are commonly invited to participate. Since their overall knowledge of office operations is limited, most employees can only take their own jobs as the subject for study and improvement. In the more *formalized* approach, an employee (or sometimes more than one employee) is given the assignment of making improvements as a part of his regular job. Specific, troublesome record-keeping projects are usually selected for study. Also, the general principles of time-and-motion study may be employed, in an effort to set work standards.

Another investigative tool employed by many *formal* work-simplification programs is the concept of motion economy. This involves breaking down useful body movements and establishing ideal work conditions. The following twelve motion-economy principles serve as guides in attempting to simplify or even completely routinize high-volume clerical jobs:

1. Move both hands simultaneously as much as possible, to perform extra work.
2. Utilize knees or feet in place of hands, where possible, to move levers, depress treadles, and so forth.
3. Employ balanced body movements—one movement should offset another.
4. Whenever possible, use rotary motions of hands or feet, bending wrists or ankles to avoid moving entire limbs.
5. Employ symmetrical or curved motions to avoid sharp changes in direction.

6. Change work patterns as often as possible to minimize fatigue or tension.
7. Work around a fixed body position, after selection of the most efficient pose.
8. Select the most convenient workplace for performance of every job. Organize the work facilities as much as possible.
9. Arrange the workplace so that a minimum of lifting or carrying is required.
10. Provide the most efficient way to dispose of finished work—a chute or moving belt may be advisable.
11. Reduce the distance between work stations to the greatest possible degree, so that transportation time is held to a minimum.
12. Improve the working environment (heat, light, sound, and ventilation) to the greatest possible extent.

With either the formal or informal type of work simplification, the major portion of the effort will normally be made as a "sideline," by employees with other prime duties. Their focus of attention will mostly be *present* record-keeping systems, procedures, or methods. This relatively narrow view is a natural concomitant of the technique employed; therefore, it is probable that *no major policies will be attacked.* In other words, *change* (rather than *elimination*) is likely to be the watchword.

In growing offices where work-simplification practices have been utilized for a considerable length of time, two important traits are universally noticeable: *orderliness* and *mechanization.* Orderliness, or lack of clutter, is actually a basic simplification technique in itself. Experienced office administrators can fully appreciate that neatness will generally go hand in hand with working efficiency. In particular, reference is being made to the *planned* kind of orderliness, which results, for example, from the installation of a sorting rack to be used by workers assembling multi-page documents. There are many other work-simplification ideas that will help in cleaning up office untidiness. You may have already developed some ideas of your own.

Formal Systems Study and Improvement

This more comprehensive (and more expensive) approach features an investigation of the objectives, assigned responsibilities, and record-keeping routines existing throughout the office. It is a more refined approach to systems analysis and usually involves the creation of a staff of full-time systems experts assigned to (1) devise large-scale changes in record-keeping, and (2) recommend changes in business policy when necessary. With this type of staff assistance, the true systems specialist comes into his own, and you, as manager of a growing office, would be well advised to remain in the role of overseer. The practice of comprehensive systems analysis involves a number of techniques that are beyond the scope of this book. Thus, the description of this approach is necessarily very brief.

The achievements to be expected from a formal systems-study program can range from very minor changes in office procedures to completely new policy and procedural concepts. Note that in such a program the emphasis is most likely to be placed on *elimination* (rather than on *change*, as in a work-simplification program).

This shift in emphasis requires the full-time effort of one or more professionals. Thus it introduces another reason why an office manager should act as a counterweight in the systems-study effort rather than attempt to participate actively. It is healthy for any organization to employ a group engaged in critical analysis of current practices, but it is also necessary for *another element* to exert a guiding or controlling influence on this analysis. As an office manager, you certainly would be the person best qualified to perform in the latter capacity. By evaluating and appraising potential system changes and by rejecting those which are not really beneficial, you can perform a valuable service which enhances the contribution provided by the systems-study group.

As an office manager, you will become involved in considering the ideal relationship between the forces of change and elimination on the one hand, and the forces of control and conservation on the other. As you make decisions, keep in mind that top management is almost entirely dependent on procedures and on information supplied by data-processing systems as the background for its decisions and plans. To summarize, the office manager's responsibility is to *furnish the needed information*. The systems analyst's responsibility is to determine *the most efficient way to accomplish this*. In the author's opinion, neither group can profitably invade the other's area of responsibility.

Systems Manuals

The final result of any type of systems improvement should be a write-up that outlines the changes. If this is properly done, various workers throughout the growing office will use it as the basis for a modification of their day-to-day jobs. For that reason, an office manager has a very considerable stake in what is written, and in how the write-up is distributed. This is one area in particular where you, as manager, need to collaborate closely with the person or team charged with studying the system.

For simplicity's sake, any written material of this nature will be referred to as a "manual." Long before a single word is written, one basic decision should be made: What is the proposed *purpose* of the manual? Will it be used as a *training aid* in introducing a new way of processing certain data? Or, will it be primarily a *reference source* for long-term or continuous use? The selection of a method of writing should be greatly influenced by this decision, and you should certainly have a considerable voice in the final decision. It is an unfortunate fact that staff groups engaged in systems analysis believe themselves to be highly qualified to make such decisions *alone*; and, in one sense, they are. However, in spite of their best intentions, if they proceed without guidance from you, the manual will inevitably be conditioned to a large extent by *problems of writing* it. In other words, the staff group will write the manual in a way that is easiest for them. The focus should instead be on *problems of using* the instructions. Obviously, having clear instructions is important both to you and to the entire office organization. Below are discussions of two common forms of instructions.

Playscript Procedural Instructions

This type of instructional material is primarily intended to be used as a *training aid*. If properly prepared, it should basically tell *who* takes *what* action *when* in the systems cycle. In the author's opinion, this structural approach is far superior to the less organized type of instruction that was never planned but "just grew" as an office training tool. The reason for this superiority is rooted in the definition of the word "procedure," meaning *to perform an action or process*. A "playscript" instruction is intended simply to tell how and when an action is to be performed.

Random samples of instructions used by a growing office such as yours will typically contain many different types of material. For example, these might include:

Various statements of policy
Definitions of important business terms and conditions
Explanations of the purpose of business activities
Descriptions of the "boundaries" of procedures
Instructions as to how and when to proceed

Of these, only the last item is a legitimate subject for the playscript procedural write-up. To be useful, every playscript write-up should begin at the inception of a system or procedural cycle and should describe all required processing in *chronological steps*. The end of the cycle and the end of the instructions must always coincide. Great emphasis is commonly placed on actions and action words (such as "start" and "take"). Also, the subject of each action must be clearly indicated. The two basic terms "subject" and "action" describe essentially all that is involved in a playscript instruction.

Functional-Outline Instructions

This form of instruction is far more useful as a *reference source* than its cousin, the playscript. It can also serve your growing office as a training aid, but here it is not as useful as a playscript, because of the volume of information that it contains. There are two other fundamental differences between functional-outline instructions and playscripts. First of all, a functional-outline type contains *policy* statements in addition to procedural descriptions. Secondly, a functional outline *completely* describes the responsibilities of a given function before passing to the next. This is entirely different from the skeletonized description found in a playscript.

A particular activity may be involved in several widely separated stages of a system cycle. For example, the "billing" function in a sales order cycle may first provide past-credit data, when the order is being considered for acceptance. Of course, the order will later be utilized in the actual billing and may serve as the source of information for collection followup. The functional-outline procedural write-up would consider *all these functions together* in the same section (although still in chronological sequence) before proceeding to the next function. A playscript, in contrast, would describe each process *as it takes place.* In other words, with a playscript, each action of the "billing" function is described in its proper time sequence, with no regard for functional relationships.

It has been the author's experience that a functional-outline manual can provide benefits to a growing office for a longer time than a playscript manual. However, that will be true *only if manuals are kept up to date,* which means a continuing cost. You'll need to decide for yourself about this, but remember— an obsolete manual may be worse than nothing at all. It very carefully and precisely tells the office staff to do something that is no longer acceptable.

Management of Business Forms

If you could select one yardstick for the measurement of business progress, it might well be the business form. In this day and age, every growing business is erected on a foundation of paper. If the paperwork props deteriorate in quality or quantity, an organization might approach collapse. On the other hand, if the quality of its paperwork can be improved, a business can be strengthened. Today, you and every other American citizen are certainly familiar with forms of many kinds. Records begin to be created for us as soon as we are born; our individual paper trails are gradually widened and lengthened as we enter school, graduate, and begin to develop our adult careers. Furthermore, the paperwork image of a person will always outlive him. Various forms recording information about him and his possessions will still be in use for months or even years after his death.

As it is with each of us personally, so it is with the business concerns where we earn our living. Here, too, forms and records are an essential part of every kind of activity, from the inception of a business until, perhaps, a bankruptcy court has completed its final action.

Definition of a Form

Despite nearly universal familiarity with the subject, there is usually a degree of vagueness about the exact meaning of the term "form." For example, you might consider a label, or an instruction booklet, or an advertising circular to be a "form"; however, the author would not. For our present purposes, a form will be defined as a card, sheet, or continuous strip of paper used for some record-keeping purpose. As much "constant" (or repetitive) information as possible will be preprinted in appropriate locations. The form will contain spaces for the entry of additional information. It may contain a reproducing "master" from which additional copies can be made. It may be used either singly or as a manifold set of various numbers of copies. It may also require the entry of nonwritten data in the form of punched holes. (The well-known "tab" card is the best example of this kind of form.)

The Cost of Forms

In seeking to control forms, *one should be primarily interested in their costs.* This interest should be much more than just an extension of general cost-consciousness on the part of the office manager. A prime factor governing general office costs is the way in which forms usage is controlled. Thus, there should be a deliberate focusing of attention on the expense of forms, in the light of their overall importance. In the author's opinion, forms control is one of the most misunderstood of all office cost-control elements.

An office form is a tangible entity—it has substance, and it may be measured, counted, or weighed. Many people, in considering the cost of forms, compute only the cost of physically producing the documents. The average office worker usually considers a blank office form to be a fairly costly item in itself. In reality, however, although the form may look expensive and although the craftspeople who produced it may be highly paid, the total cost for paper and printing will never amount to more than a few cents per form. This common misconception about the costliness of the unprocessed form itself, coupled with the normal tendency to underrate the expense of clerical labor, creates confusion about *where* the emphasis on form cost control should be placed. Actually, an unprepared (blank) form might be compared to a raw piece of sheet steel that is ready to be run through a punch press, thus beginning a fabricating operation. *The cost has hardly begun to be incurred at this point.* However, as soon as the blank form begins to be handled, to receive entries, to be separated into various parts, to be distributed, to be read, to be audited, to be filed—in short, as soon as the form is placed in use—then its cost begins to mount significantly.

With these thoughts in mind, we can better understand that the most important aspect of forms cost is *not* related to the size or kind of paper and ink from which a form is made.

The real expense is determined largely by *the amount of time employees spend in working with the form*. If you want to promote more efficient use of a form, or have a record prepared mechanically instead of by hand, or eliminate completely one step of preparation, you'll automatically produce a saving in form costs. On the other hand, if you decide to begin a stringent program to pinch pennies by cheapening the grade of paper for the form, or by having the form duplicated instead of printed, or by initiating any other so-called printing economy measure, you could actually be increasing costs, even though the blank form itself will be less expensive. As a result, when office forms control is discussed in this book, our attention will *not* be directed primarily toward the physical attributes of forms, except as these affect the form's use. If a particular characteristic *enhances the use of a form*, it is to be recommended. If not, it is better avoided.

The Relationship of Forms to Computerized Record-Keeping

As discussed in the next chapter, the age of computers is upon us. If your office hasn't taken the plunge as yet, it will probably happen before long. In some way and to a moderate or a considerable extent, some of your office procedures have been or will be converted to the use of electronic data processing. Therefore, we should briefly consider the effect of office automation on record-keeping forms. Note that automation, by its very nature, must be applied only to *high-volume* record-keeping work. Thus, the *number of different forms* that are affected by automation will normally be small.

Record-keeping forms used with automated systems will usually possess two general characteristics:

1. They will be relatively complex in construction and will demand rigid control over technical specifications. The mechanical limitations imposed by automated forms-handling equipment will not permit variances.

2. With automation, some records or segments of records will actually be eliminated altogether, since so much more computation or record-keeping is carried on internally by the

computer. Perhaps the best example of this is the common practice of storing sizable amounts of information on punched tape, magnetic tape, or floppy discs; each of these serves an an electronic "memory." This mode of storage completely eliminates many ledger cards and/or punched cards that might otherwise be needed.

About three-fourths of your office forms, however, will probably be totally unaffected by the computer, since these forms will not be incorporated as a part of an automated system. For that reason, too much emphasis should not be placed on the subject. The less glamorous but much more numerous *regular* type of record-keeping forms will continue as the mainstay of your office forms-control program.

Responsibility for Forms Control

Sooner or later, we must face the specific question of *who in the office is to be responsible for forms control*? Should you, as office manager, be assigned this duty? Or, if not, why not? The question begins to answer itself when we start to consider exactly what the term "forms control" really means. Speaking broadly, forms control involves all steps required to provide the record-keeping documents an office needs to conduct its business. It also includes the responsibility for eliminating forms that become obsolete. Finally, forms control certainly must encompass the duty of revising existing forms in order to improve their effectiveness, meet special data requirements, or make them conform to changed conditions. In greater detail, forms control should cover the following specific activities:

1. Investigating the use of each record-keeping form, to ensure that it fulfills some real requirement of the organization
2. Designing the layout of each form to permit maximum efficiency of preparation and also ease of later use
3. Specifying the most economical but also the most desirable materials for the form; in addition, determining in general how the form will be manufactured

4. Ensuring that the proper provision is made for replenishing the stock of forms at some future time, if this should be necessary

In the author's opinion, the above description of minimum forms-control duties should be sufficient to indicate that any manager of a growing office *cannot be held directly responsible* for the function. Time would not permit fulfillment of this duty along with the office manager's many other regular assignments. Instead, it is suggested that this staff function be separately assigned, and that the office manager's responsibility be related to it in the same measure and to the degree as already discussed in connection with systems analysis.

The Relation of Office Management to Forms Control

The author's recommendation is to avoid a *direct* linking of responsibility between forms control and office administration. However, this is not meant to imply there should be no connection whatever. That would be both ridiculous and impossible. Since forms constitute a tool and also a by-product of office work, there *must* be a close tie-in. The problem is to determine how to make the connection.

The author would recommend that an office manager utilize forms control in the same way that one might seek the services of a medical doctor. The analogy is not completely applicable, however, since we do not normally employ a doctor to *keep us well*. And that is precisely how forms control should act in relationship to office management. Any improper form design or construction should be detected and corrected *before* it can do much harm—in other words, before the office has a "sick" record-keeping system.

You will often find it within your power to ensure that forms-control personnel have adequate leeway to operate satisfactorily. In fact, it has been the author's experience that office managers in growing companies usually promote forms control, simply for their own good. That could be the case in your organization. Since office management generally derives most of the benefit from good forms control, this simply makes sense.

Some Forms-Control Processes

Like so many human activities, forms control has no absolute rules. Instead, it will vary among different offices. Furthermore, in some business concerns the control may be exercised in a very meticulous fashion, whereas in others a much more casual approach is taken. The author believes, however, that very few progressive and expanding organizations today can completely ignore the need for forms control.

No matter how extensively a forms-control program is enforced—and regardless of whether it is a weak or strong effort—the program usually includes (1) forms-numbering and (2) forms design. These processes serve important purposes *outside the forms-control group itself.* In other words, they are more than mere devices that are intended to be exclusively utilized for internal control activities. Forms-numbering and forms design are discussed below.

Forms-Numbering

Although the practice of assigning an identifying number to each separate form is considered to be mandatory for control purposes, it is of equal value for the *users* of the forms. The following benefits are provided by a proper numbering system:

1. *Identification* of each form
2. Indication of *different uses* or purposes
3. Designation of *old* or *new* versions

One or all of some intermediate combination of these benefits can be obtained for your office, depending on the desired complexity of the numbering plan. For example, the form number 1234 serves only to identify the form. To supply slightly more information, a prefix such as E (for employee) or C (for cost) can be added for identification. Actually, it is usually preferable to use a *number* rather than a *letter* for identification of a business process or activity since the variety of activities will sooner or later exceed the number of letters in the alphabet. Thus, a cost form might be identified as 17–1234; in this case, 17 signifies "cost," and 1234 identifies the form. To carry the example still further, we might inject an indication of the use or purpose of the form. In such a case, the "cost" form could also contain a suffix to signify "report." The more complicated "cost report" form number might then appear as 17–1234–09. Taking a different tack, we could add a revision date behind the identifying number to indicate whether the form has an old or new style. Thus: 1234 (1–84).

It should be apparent that any of your employees who is acquainted with the selected code can obtain fairly valuable information from a form number alone, without even inspecting the form which bears that number. The potential benefit that could reasonably be expected from using certain codes would depend entirely on your own office situation. You should certainly try to achieve either maximum *simplicity* or greatest *utility* in a form number, whichever fits the needs of the office. In setting up a code system for forms identification, one basic fact should never be overlooked: the longer the form number, the more digits will have to be written, typed, or machine-printed each time the form is ordered, received, requisitioned, referred to, or otherwise processed.

Forms Design

While efficient forms design is almost exclusively the concern of the forms-control staff, the *results* of this design effort will directly affect the work of the office. Various office personnel will be handicapped or helped by a particular form layout, by various arrangements of copies, and by other design properties. This in turn will have a direct bearing on the efficiency and profitability of office operations. Therefore, although you can do little except look over the shoulder of a forms designer, this kibitzing may take the shape of helpful suggestions for improvement. You can also offer a pointed reminder when a new or revised form has characteristics that may hamper efficiency.

Because of every office manager's probable interest in the matter, forms-design principles will be discussed briefly. However, bear in mind the author's recommendation that the office manager should *not* participate in actual design work. To be able to distinguish well-designed forms from those that are poorly designed ought to be sufficient for the office manager's purposes. To do more would be to surrender the functions of an administrator in favor of those of a technician.

There is no profound mystery to good forms design. The hallmarks are readily apparent, so long as one fundamental fact is well understood—that is, *a form should be easy to use*. It should lend itself to efficient preparation, and there should be sufficient space for all entries. It should permit rapid abstracting or copying of information. The arrangement of the entries ought to be established with these principles in mind. Any instructions for completing the form ought to be prominently displayed on the form and in a standard location. The paper on which the form is printed should be of a color, weight, and strength that are consistent with its manner of use. The way in which copies of the form are glued or stapled together must permit rapid preparation and separation. Enough copies, but not too many, should be provided to permit all departments concerned to obtain required data.

A comprehensive list of good forms-design characteristics can be used as a guide in evaluating any particular form. Such a list would include the following points:

1. *Form heading*. All forms should have titles for identification and to describe their function. The title should be centered at the top or bottom of the sheet. Enough space should be allowed to give balance to the form's appearance. Important references such as significant names or numbers should be placed in the upper-right or upper-left corner for prominence.

2. *Form body*. If a certain kind of office machine is to be used in form preparation, areas for entries should be of the right size to conform to the spacing of the machine. Typed entries should be arranged in horizontal alignment, insofar as possible, so that a minimum of vertical spacing will be re-

quired. Also, entries should not be "staggered" in different locations across the sheet. Columnar arrangement should be used instead. Where possible, use labor-saving ideas such as "check boxes," elimination of a vertical line separating dollar entries from cent entries, and folding guidelines.

3. *Foot of the form.* Entries should *not* be required too close to the bottom, since this makes it impossible to use a machine for these entries. The lower section can be used for other things, however. It is the most desirable area for form numbers, names of persons or departments that will receive copies, and instructions for filling out the form.

Although the above points barely scratch the surface of the subject of forms design, they are adequate for our present purposes.

To sum up the kind of service that you can reasonably expect properly designed forms to perform, the author recommends that every form should give necessary directions, supply required data, and generally help to ensure that the record system of which it is a part will be maintained. Coordination with the forms-control group will certainly be necessary to ensure that all office forms actually do perform such services.

Conclusion

The purpose of this chapter has been to explore ways in which systems study and forms management can provide improved cost control and contribute to profitable office operations generally. So much attention has been devoted to this subject because the prime function of office management is to provide records and reports that will serve as grist for the management mills. Every member of the business administration depends on such information. There can be no planning, no controlling, no managerial functions without the kinds of data that an office turns out.

Therefore, it is appropriate to say that the better use which an office manager makes of the staff support services that are furnished by systems study and forms management, the more profitably the company can operate. It's as simple as that.

8
Your Office of Tomorrow Could Be Here Today

There are several ways in which the author could begin a discussion about the rapidly expanding scope of electronic data processing and its probable impact on your office. One approach would be to describe the marvels of the newly available "hardware" (the term which is used to describe the equipment itself) and "software" (a way of referring to preestablished computer programs that can be obtained in profusion to cover virtually every large-scale clerical activity performed in modern offices). But this would be like writing a treatise on irrigation while sitting in a rowboat in the middle of a Mississippi flood. All that water could change anyone's perspective, and so many recent developments in the field of electronics are equally overwhelming. Furthermore, between the time when these lines are written, and the day when you are reading the printed book, many additional new products and concepts unquestionably will be devised and put into use. Since the chapter can't include such novelties, it will be out of date from the beginning.

However, in the author's opinion, if you want to understand what's going on, you don't need a list of "gee whiz" features as much as you need a discussion of principles. The latter will stay the same much longer; the life span of special features becomes shorter and shorter as our technological revolution continues. That's what we're living in—a time when new ideas come out of someone's brain and are put to practical use at such a rapid rate that many people become intimidated. If you can ignore the feeling that most of what you know is about to become obsolete (which is probably what will happen unless you take positive measures to prevent it), and instead determine to stay up to date (which isn't as difficult as it sounds), then you and your office will survive. You might even do better than that; you could prosper.

The Importance of Proper Facilities

Before we launch into an examination of the technically innovative side of the office of tomorrow, it will pay to walk out into your office and simply look around. Does the place have a shabby look? Is it cluttered? Are the equipment and furniture rather worn? Does it *seem to be inefficient*? You may be so familiar with the office that you can't view it dispassionately. After all, it's your second home; you're used to it. Consider asking someone else to take a critical look.

"Contemporary" offices have two common characteristics—they generally are fairly efficient and what's more, *they usually look as if they are*. However, if your office is similar to most of those which the author encounters, its appearance is much less impressive than that. Perhaps you have a few modern touches—some equipment or furnishings recently acquired—but, by and large, your office work environment is probably about the same as it was five years ago. So, to move into the future, the first thing to consider should be the physical characteristics of your office.

Office Layout

Today, the concept of effective layout is widely understood. Many children attend functionally designed schools. New homes often feature a "zoning" design, with locales for different activities being separated according to a strict plan, and with the kitchen resembling an assembly line. Some public buildings display a "clean" look, with easy-to-understand direction signs, wide aisles, a lack of partitions, and contemporary accoutrements. All of these updated interior arrangements represent efficiency—a better way to learn or live or work. Now let's turn to your office and consider *its layout*.

Proper space allocation. In reviewing how your office space is allocated, there are three factors which warrant consideration. One is the *present workload* assigned to each office department or section. The next is *possible future changes* in that volume of work. The final factor to be considered is the *existence of important interoffice* (or intraoffice) *relationships*: Should Step 1 in a sequential series of operations be as close as possible to Step 2, or doesn't it matter much? A systematic analysis of working arrangements throughout the entire office is needed if these three factors are to be given proper importance. The volume of paper flow, the desired level of output, and the working contacts among office employees—all are important. The author has found that a combined work-flow diagram, depicting all major systems cycles, is a good way to begin. Such a diagram illustrates *functional relationships* quite clearly. It also provides a reasonably good indication of work-volume. The next analytical step is to consider the *number of people*, since every worker requires at least the minimum square footage of working space. Other matters to be considered are *future business expansion* and, of course, the *total size* of the available area.

It isn't absolutely essential to follow any preferred plan of analysis in surveying an office. The most important thing is to eventually arrive at the correct answer—at least for the present—and to compare it with existing arrangements.

Planning of office layouts. If you conclude either (1) that the present layout is seriously inefficient, or (2) that the future is likely to make it that way, then the next step is to try to introduce some changes. Many guidelines have been established, governing the way in which an "office of tomorrow" ought to be laid out. If you want your office to have that thoroughly modern look, here are some points to be considered:

• The latest trend in office arrangement features an "open" office with very few solid, permanent partitions reaching from floor to ceiling. The only exception to such a rule is that one or more conference rooms will be needed. The latter should be used for large or disruptive gatherings or for those occasions when a truly private meeting or discussion must be held.

• Thus, the first step in planning a contemporary layout must be to subdivide the available space between that reserved for general office use, and the smaller areas reserved for a conference room or rooms.

• General work areas are then planned to be "broken up" by the introduction of movable, shoulder-high partitions. These serve as boundaries between different office functions, and are also used for privacy. One noticeable feature of modern offices is the multiplicity of cubicles partitioned off by the shoulder-high barriers and reserved for occupancy by one or two workers.

Arrangement of office furniture. The actual location of furniture or equipment in a redesigned office should be consistent with work-efficiency requirements. Most manufacturers of movable partitions also provide various convenience items that can be attached to or hung directly on the partitions in order to serve as file cabinets, bookcases, credenzas, and so forth. This is a very effective use of space and is certainly recommended (if you can afford it). Other common-sense rules governing office furniture are as follows:

• Workers seated at desks or equipment should not face a window or other source of glare.
• When furniture or equipment is grouped, workers should not face one another. Instead, if possible, they should all face the same direction. If someone in the group is "in charge," that person should be located to one side of or (preferably) behind the remainder of the workers.
• Tables, desks, and equipment located in large open areas should be arranged in straight lines. Sufficient and uniform aisle width should be maintained.

- Desks in cubicles should either face the doorway or be to one side of the door. A worker should not be seated with a doorway to his back.
- Adequate seating should be provided for people or groups of people who typically come into a cubicle to confer with the occupant.
- Noisy equipment should be isolated behind a floor-to-ceiling partition.
- Vending machines, coatracks, drinking fountains, bulletin boards, and other employee conveniences should be located away from working areas.

The efficiency of orderly appearance. Clutter is out of date. If you want to be modern, strive for neatness and uniformity.

Next time you have the opportunity to see an example of the "office of tomorrow"—either at a business show, in illustrations from a magazine, or the real thing, an actual working office—notice how tidy it seems. All the furniture is the same size and shape. The arrangement is quite orderly. There are no open ledger tubs, no stacks of folders on top of files. There is a place for everything, and everything is where it belongs.

If you accept the principle that order and efficiency go hand in hand, you will have taken a long step toward the office of the future. It's probable that you can't spend enough money to convert your office overnight into the twenty-first century. However, it doesn't cost very much to achieve a neat appearance. In fact, a simple coat of paint and updated light fixtures will take you quite a distance. Let's consider the benefits that these relatively inexpensive features can bring to a growing office.

Office Environmental Improvements

It isn't the author's intent to undertake a technical discussion of the heating or cooling or lighting in your office. There will be no references to office decor or to color combinations. The purpose of this section is simply to present environmental requirements in a general, nontechnical way in order to help you recognize any poor conditions that might exist in your office. Then, if changes are needed, you can consult an expert.

Ventilation, heating, and cooling of the office. Disputes over wages or working hours can create much personnel conflict; so can the temperature of an office. If you accept the statement that an average human being is most comfortable when the thermometer stands at about 72° F, then you may come to believe that very few workers in your office are average. Usually, women seem to prefer temperatures higher than 72° F, while men often like it cooler than that. If there is to be a future "battle of the sexes," it could very well occur in the vicinity of the air conditioner control or the radiator knob.

Actually, the modern approach to heating, cooling, and ventilating an office features a "zoned" plan. Temperature variations are most noticeable in those parts of the office closest to sources of heat or cold. In many offices, the zone of temperature extremes occurs around the outer edge of the room, where vents or windows admit cold drafts in the winter and heat in the summer. Thus, if you want the office to be as comfortable as most people's homes, consider a perimeter of about fifteen feet back from the outside as a *separate zone.* The temperature-control system serving this area should be able to provide warm or cool air more effectively than in any other part of the office. By taking such an approach, you may even find that only ventilating measures are needed for the remaining interior areas.

Don't discount the importance of the office "climate." Poor conditions will have a direct, negative impact on morale and also on office output. If the temperature in the office goes too high or too low, or if the humidity of the air is uncomfortable, absenteeism will increase; time lost due to actual illness will also grow. Modern office workers will refuse to accept environmental conditions that would not have been considered so unsatisfactory fifty years ago. It's up to you to be constantly on the lookout for heating, cooling, or ventilating problems, and to correct them where possible.

Office lighting. Most office jobs involve "seeing" work. That is the reason why the office of tomorrow will provide more and better light directed toward the workplace. Lighting devices have become more efficient and also more versatile over the years. There is an increased realization that efficient performance requires optimum visibility. You are no doubt aware from personal experience that the human eye can adjust to inadequate light. Possibly you might not even realize that some jobs in your office aren't properly illuminated. However, such situations bring on eye fatigue and result in more mistakes. It's your responsibility to identify poor lighting conditions and to have them corrected. The result will be more profitable operations, and you'll be closer to the goal of a truly modern office.

Two factors contribute to office illumination: "brightness" and "contrast." Proper lighting affects both. When you are seeking better visibility of work, you should be aware that *quantity of light* (brightness) is not the only necessity. The presence of moderate contrasts is also crucial—in other words, the *quality of light*. While every opportunity should be made to take advantage of natural daylight, special effort is required to avoid the glare of the sun. Remember that light quantity is dependent on the source alone, but light quality is conditioned by many things within the office that produce glare or contrast such as shiny desk tops, sunny windows, or vividly colored objects.

The office of tomorrow will feature three different forms of lighting, each designed for special purposes. These unique approaches to office lighting are readily available today:

1. *Indirect lighting* is most desirable for actual working areas. It is as close as you'll be able to come to natural daylight, with freedom from glare or shadows. Properly designed light fixtures aim most of the light upward toward a reflective surface, with the remainder of the light directed to the sides.
2. *Semi-indirect lighting* is appropriate for corridors, conference rooms, and other sections of the office where little to moderate amounts of clerical work take place. With this type, some of the light is cast downward, while

the remainder goes up or to the sides. Not as many light fixtures are needed, but mild shadows may be noticed and illumination is less than perfect.

3. *Direct lighting* means that virtually all of the light is directed downward, or onto a target area. Strong shadows and glare can occur. This type of lighting should be confined to reception rooms, or to particular uses such as illumination of displays or charts. In other words, direct lighting should be used sparingly and only to provide concentrated light when needed.

One other lighting feature will be used to an increasing degree in the office of tomorrow: variable controls will permit light levels to be raised or lowered at will, in closely adjacent sections of the office. For example, maximum lighting can be provided for a group of workers using some type of equipment, while only partial light can be used a few feet away where other members of the staff are watching a training film. Moderate perimeter light around the edges of a conference room can be amplified where needed, to allow increased visibility for some type of display that the conference leader plans to use as the center of attention. The possibilities are endless. The prime ingredient for improvement is the office manager's appreciation of different light uses.

Before leaving this subject, we need to say a few words about color and reflectivity. Brightness (the quantity of light) is directly affected by the reflection of light from various surfaces, and also by the color of such surfaces. Light colors bounce back more light than do dark tones. Highly polished surfaces can produce glare; dull surfaces do not. Since offices can be repainted for much less than the expense of remodeling, and since the color and shininess of a painted surface have little effect on what redecoration would cost, the lighting of an office can be greatly improved by using some of the proper kinds and colors of paint.

Office sounds control. Many kinds of office work create noise as a by-product. Too much noise produces fatiguing side effects for every worker within hearing distance. In contrast, the use of pleasant sounds can provide a welcome background for workers who are engaged in monotonous work. For these two reasons, the office of tomorrow will feature many sound-control devices. You can move in the same direction.

Irritating office noise can either be absorbed or isolated. Some materials used in ceilings, floors, walls, and partitions will dramatically reduce noise levels. Such materials generally are "soft": that is, they have qualities which resemble a sponge, and excessive noise seems almost to be "soaked up" by their surfaces. Other materials, which are hard and shiny, have the opposite effect. Noise rebounds and, in fact, seems to be amplified. Have you ever noticed the difference in sounds when a group of women wearing high-heeled shoes walk from a tile or terrazzo surface onto a carpeted area?

The isolation of noise can be handled in different ways, depending on the degree of irritation. Use of shoulder-high partitions (discussed earlier) will break up sound patterns. Then, if these partitions are surfaced with cloth or some other noise-absorbent material, the total effect is remarkable. On the other hand, really excessive noise must be shut off completely from other office areas. A floor-to-ceiling partition, permanently installed, is the best remedy.

A surprising amount of office noise can also be successfully counteracted by music played over a public address system. If the noise is fairly loud, try turning the music volume up enough to make the latter audible. If the office is rather quiet, the music should be more subdued. You may not be aware of how effectively music can be used to "mask" a noisy office.

Technical Advances Affecting Office Processes

There are three prime innovations that will be featured in offices of tomorrow, and that can have a profound effect on growing offices today. These are the small business computer, the word processor, and teleconferencing. Since the small computer represents the "foundation" for change, it will be discussed first. The other two improvements represent special capabilities of these versatile small computing devices, which you should definitely investigate (if you haven't already). Therefore, we'll round out this section by examining the potential profitability of word processors and teleconferencing for your office.

The Computer Is Coming, the Computer Is Coming!

An estimated one-fifth of all office workers—mostly employed in large offices—now use cathode ray tube terminals (CRTs) as part of their equipment at work. By the late 1980s, this tool will have increased enough in popularity so that *half of the office working force* in this country will be making regular use of it. Improvement in the technology of electronic data storage and retrieval will make this not only possible but mandatory. Shouldn't you learn something *now* about this forthcoming revolution?

Back in the early 1970s, the author was manager of corporate systems for a Fortune-500-sized corporation. The main frame computer that we were using for corporate-level data processing at that time had considerably less computing power than does a typical small business computer that you can examine today at a computer "store" in a shopping center. Furthermore, the cost of computers has declined so rapidly that a dollar today buys as much as $1,000 did fifteen years ago. Because of their low cost, small size, and substantial computing power, these small business computers will soon be everywhere. Growing businesses of all types will be induced to enter the "computer age," by the force of competition if not a desire for progress. To provide you with an overview, we will present a "quick and dirty" look at what a computer consists of and how it works. Don't be intimidated by technical jargon. You need not understand any of the inner workings of these devices in order to be able to put one to use.

1. *Output.* This is what a computer provides you as the payoff. You can get information retrieved from the computer's "memory". You can get the solution to a problem. You can also get the computer's "best guess" as to what will happen in the

future. Any output data can either be printed on paper or shown on a CRT screen.

2. *Input.* This is what you communicate to the computer, so that it can process the information. You need to input instructions, and also a variety of numeric or alphabetic characters. The input process may be carried out by using a keyboard very similar to a typewriter, or by inserting a preprogrammed disk into a reading device.

3. *Memory.* This is the electromechanical feature that has enabled computers to take on an almost human quality. Computers are able to retain "raw" information, "processed" information, and also the complete set of instructions that you provide, detailing what you want the computer to do and how.

4. *Arithmetic unit.* This single-purpose element of the computer can do nothing but add, subtract, multiply, divide, and take square roots. (Actually, multiplication is a special form of adding, while division and square root calculations are unique forms of subtraction.) The computer can perform these functions, using binary arithmetic, so rapidly that the speed is almost unbelievable.

5. *Central processor.* This might be called the "switchboard" of the computer, because everything must be processed through it. However, the central processor is also the controller, taking your data, your instructions, and information already in memory, and putting everything to use in the way you have specified. As an example, the central processor will sit and wait until signaled to begin, then instruct the computer memory to provide data to the arithmetic unit. The latter then performs the proper calculation and passes the answer back to the controller. The controller takes the final step of notifying the output device to provide you with the result you need, either in printed form or as symbols on a screen.

The above information is very skeletal; the purpose in providing it has only been to take away some of the "black magic" that has become associated with computers in the minds of the general public. What you really need to understand is how a computer can help your office.

Computer applications. There are literally hundreds of

"canned" programs, developed for the family of small computers and sitting on a shelf waiting to be put to use. Through proper application of this computer software, you can write a payroll, bill a customer, pay your suppliers, maintain perpetual inventory records, compute product cost, and so on and so on. Someone in your office needs to know only how to turn on the computer, insert a disk or two, and tell it to get to work.

Computer literacy. If you want your office to go beyond merely keeping records on a computer in a preestablished way (as described above), then someone in the office must become computer-literate. That means, he or she will have learned how to "talk" to the computer so that it can be told to do something unique or different. To say it another way, being computer-literate is knowing how to write a program or how to utilize existing software.

Computer training. Don't even think of investing in a small business computer until you determine that you can train several people to use it. To do otherwise would be the equivalent of buying a shiny new truck when no one in the office has a driver's license. Many "computer stores" and computer manufacturers will be clamoring for your money. Not nearly as many will be able to teach one or more of your workers how to use the thing after it is set up in your office. Some will have a booklet with "easy, step-by-step directions that anyone can understand." Others will say, "Just call us on the phone; we'll help get you straightened out." Baloney. What your people will need will be classroom, hands-on training. At least twenty hours of it is required to get the average beginner under way. At the end of that time, employees will have begun to be able to program, will know how to use software, and, last but not least, will no longer be afraid of that threatening collection of hardware which cost you several thousands of dollars.

Word Processors Can Be "Secretary-Friendly"

Producing accurate, edited typed copy is never easy. Some secretaries find it far more troublesome than others; that is particularly true if they have a nitpicker for a boss. Yet with a word processor, a secretary-and-boss team can collaborate to produce perfect letters or manuscript in a fraction of the time that would be needed otherwise. A word processor is simply an electronic typewriter with a memory, hitched to a small computer. Here's how a typical installation could work:

1. The boss dictates into a regular telephone, which is part of the system.
2. The secretary later listens to a recording of that dictation, using a headset with earphones. She types what she hears, which goes into the system's temporary memory.
3. When the boss is ready, he or she tells a CRT to display the typing on the screen. The boss then types final changes into a computer keyboard.
4. The word processor corrects spelling, arranges the length of lines of type, and prints out a final draft.
5. The secretary then "files" the text of the material in permanent memory and gives the boss the typed product.

Sounds great, doesn't it? Unfortunately, there are other ways to use work processors that are less inspiring. A word processor can produce a single final draft or it can produce a thousand of the same thing. A typist (not a secretary) can sit all day, calling different names and addresses out of memory and then telling the word processor to produce identical letters for each name and address. Talk about a bleary-eyed typist; talk about an endlessly monotonous job!

Ideal applications for word processing may or may not exist in your growing office. It depends on the size of the company and the nature of the business. If you now have a large volume of typed output or a pool of typists, it would be a very good idea to look into the prospects for an installation of this "high tech" device. But, if you do, be sure you give thorough study to the way that the new system will either mesh with or conflict with existing office activities. Otherwise, you might be disappointed by users' disinterest in the word processing service.

Why Travel When You Can Teleconference?

You may already be aware that the local phone company has a room for rent that can save many travel dollars for your company. This room is often equipped with a television camera and monitor, a two-way sound system, and possibly an "electronic blackboard." There may also be a telephone terminal for connecting with your computer back in the office. In a room like that, members of the sales force or a few key executives from your organization can talk "face to face" with clients or suppliers hundreds of miles away, who are using similar facilities rented from another phone company. This is a space-age marvel that is becoming popular very rapidly. (If the television equipment is too expensive or simply not yet available, your people could use computer terminals to exchange information without being able to see or hear the other parties. The effect isn't as dramatic as being able to watch facial expressions or hear someone's voice tones, but the result is generally about the same.)

As office manager, you may not get to participate in many teleconferences. Still, you can lead the way in convincing others to take this step. The communication of information is, after all, a function of every office. Thus, you won't be "out of line" at all in trying to promote the concept.

The Impact of Electronic Technology on Office Personnel

Despite the tremendous strides that office *equipment* manufacturers are making these days and the upheaval in office record-keeping that will result from an electronic "information explosion," the most profound change is likely to be the effect

on office *people*. Day-to-day jobs and work relationships gradually become so familiar that we tend to think of them as
permanent. Yet, many of these well-known practices will be
subject to drastic changes in the future. We will close our
discussion of your "office of tomorrow" by reflecting on some
of these shifting patterns.

How Personnel Administration May Be "Depersonalized"

It has already become possible to computerize personnel
records, and to store substantial amounts of electronic information about employee performance. With these advances in
place, the next logical step is to categorize various personal
qualities such as the interests, skills, and aptitudes of employees. Once this is done, codes can be developed for a variety
of individual traits. You no doubt can see what is coming. All
of the unique qualities that characterize a particular person
can be reduced to a series of numbers and entered into the
personnel data bank of the computer. When new jobs open
up, when promotions are being considered, when layoffs become necessary, *the computer can help select the people* who
will be affected.

How New Types of Physical Ailments Can Occur

When a worker sits all day looking at a CRT, various kinds
of discomfort occur. Headaches and visual problems, stiff necks,
and backaches are some of these. Mental strain and boredom
can also result. In other words, the electronic workplace can
expose workers to a whole new world of job hazards. In the
"old days," the author occasionally encountered a complaint
from a woman who had gotten a run in her stocking by bump-
ing into a file drawer that someone had left open. Nowadays,
there is much more likelihood that either men or women will
complain about "snow blindness," brought on by staring at
columns of numbers shifting across the face of their CRT.

How Office Jobs Can Be Performed Away from the Office

It may soon be more convenient and economical for some of your employees to sit at keyboards in their living rooms, and communicate with the office electronically. They might then be paid only for the amount of output produced, rather than for hours spent in the office. Also, office hours could be much more flexible, since an employee could start work in the middle of the night and store everything in computer memory, waiting for someone in the office to send an electronic readout signal the next day. Furthermore, the same person could be employed part-time by several offices and could complete many different assignments without ever leaving home.

The Impact of Electronic Technology on Office Management

Just as your employees will be affected by new administrative practices, so your job will also change. Prior to the advent of the computer, information processing in the office had developed around two general ground rules. First of all, data had to be transmitted either "slowly but surely" (by recording it on paper) or "rapidly but impermanently" (by verbalizing it over the phone). In either case, the transmission was extremely inefficient compared to sending electronic data via a telephone wire network. Secondly, despite much progress, data were still "difficult" to analyze, because electrical or electromechanical sorting and compiling were primitive in comparison to electronic data processing. The terms "slowly," "impermanently," and "difficult," are, of course, only relative. A great deal of time and energy have been devoted by you (and other office managers) to reducing these disadvantages. You may have speeded up data transmission and cut down on the expense of such transmission. You probably have reduced some of the difficulties of data analysis. *But you have always been handicapped by technological limitations*, until the computer came along.

Furthermore—and very importantly—the way in which

you administered and compensated the work force has also been conditioned by those same limitations. For example, your basic salary system has almost surely been based on time spent on the job, rather than on output, *because time is so much easier to measure.* And when you hired people, or trained them, or promoted them, you couldn't effectively compare individuals with diverse backgrounds. As a result, you had to hire, train, and promote according to "norms"—that is, according to what past experience and judgment had taught you to do.

When you really move into the office of tomorrow, you'll be able to capture and analyze information on a much wider scale, and with fantastic speed. That simply means that your choices of action will greatly expand. You can avoid many inefficiencies. You can stop underutilizing employees who are capable of greater productivity. You can discontinue paying people as much for work poorly done as for work well done. You can fit workers more closely into the kinds of work that they like to do. You can also prevent the retention of people in your office who are no longer able or willing to perform at the required level.

In conclusion, workers are the basis of office productivity. As the office manager develops better relationships with personnel, and better control over work costs and quality, every phase of office work becomes more efficient. Efficiency spells profitability, and greater profitability should always be your main goal.

Suggested Readings

Bittel, Lester R. *What Every Supervisor Should Know*, 4th ed. New York: McGraw-Hill, 1980.

Boje, Axel. *Open Plan Office*. London, England: Business Books, Ltd., 1971.

Heyel, Carl, ed. *Handbook of Modern Office Management and Administrative Services*. New York: McGraw-Hill, 1972.

Johnson, Thomas W. and John E. Stinson. *Managing Today and Tomorrow*. Reading, Mass.: Addison-Wesley, 1978.

Littlefield, C. L., F. M. Rachel, D. L. Caruth, and R. E. Holmes. *Management of Office Operations*. Englewood Cliffs, N.J.: Prentice-Hall, 1978.

Nance, Harold W. and Robert E. Nolan. *Office Work Measurement*. New York: McGraw-Hill, 1971.

Smith, Harold T. and William H. Baker. *The Administrative Manager*. Chicago: Science Research Associates, Inc., 1978.

Terry, George R. *Office Management and Control: The Administrative Managing of Business*. Homewood, Ill.: Richard D. Irwin, 1975.

Zaiden, Dennis J. *Dartnell's Paperwork Simplification Manual*. Chicago: Dartnell Corporation, 1974.

Index